7th April 2011

Happy 18th Hugh!

to our man who loves his roasts

All our Love

Dad x and Mum xx

Good
Old-Fashioned
Roasts

Good Old-Fashioned Roasts

Laura Mason

THE NATIONAL TRUST

Acknowledgements

With many thanks to Vivian Bullivant, Robert Byas, Ivan Day, Caroline Liddell, Jenny Whitley and Agnes Winter for good advice and good roasts; and to the editors at National Trust Books for their patience.

First published in the United Kingdom in 2009 by
National Trust Books
10 Southcombe Street
London W14 0RA

An imprint of Anova Books Ltd

Text and recipes © Laura Mason
Copyright © National Trust Books

ISBN: 9781905400720

A CIP catalogue record for this book is available from the British Library.

15 14 13 12 11 10 09 08
10 9 8 7 6 5 4 3 2 1

Printed and bound by 1010 Printing International Ltd, China
Repro by Dot Gradations Ltd, England

Photography by Tara Fisher
Home economy by Jane Suthering
Styling by Wei Tang

This book can be ordered direct from the publisher at the website: www.anovabooks.com, or try your local bookshop. Also available at National Trust shops or www.nationaltrustbooks.co.uk

Contents

Introduction

What is a roast? Much more than a hunk of meat cooked in a certain way. Think of a roast and we think of vast joints of beef turning on spits in front of huge fires, of venison poached from under the gamekeeper's nose, of medieval boards groaning under the weight of peacocks, swans and sucking pigs, of Christmas geese and turkeys, and of convivial Sunday dinners. In short, a roast is an idea of plenty, of feasting (legitimate or otherwise), and of occasion. Over the years this has been allowed to decline into the bland reality of gravy granules and ready meals.

A roast is worth more than that. Meat is a resource that is likely to become scarcer – and well-produced meat even more so. We should value it properly for what it is – a food in which months, or possibly years, of an animal's life is concentrated into a package of protein and fat, at once nourishing and delicious, an excuse for a gathering, and provider of meals to come.

Good meat for a roast is expensive and, to some extent, a luxury. This is how it should be – as, too, should be the ability to use meat left over from one meal to make another, equally appealing meal. An element of a long-held idea that British meat is so good that it needs no 'messing about' still persists, but before the 19th century strong flavours were appreciated, as they are once again. Many of the recipes given here try to capture some of the flavours of the past, using as inspiration recipes from historic cookery texts that would undoubtedly have found their way into the kitchens of houses now owned by the National Trust. Also included are a few forays into current fashions.

The Idea of the Roast

A roast forms a special part of British eating habits, even if it is not quite the weekly punctuation mark it once was. Changes in taste and lifestyle have influenced how people eat; but a well-chosen piece of meat, carefully cooked, is an opportunity for conviviality, a gathering of family and friends.

Originally, roasting meant cooking by exposing meat to radiant heat in front of an open fire. Even casual inspection of historic cookery books shows that this was considered a very important method for cooking meat (and to a lesser extent, fish). Foreigners remarked on English skill in roasting. Henri Misson, who visited from France in the early 18th century, described cookshops in London with four spits revolving one above another before a fire, each bearing 'five or six Pieces of Butcher's Meat, Beef, Mutton, Veal, Pork and Lamb'. Customers ordered meat done to their taste, and ate it with salt, mustard, bread rolls and bottles of beer. In 1747 another traveller, the Scandinavian clergyman Pehr Kalm, wrote that 'English men understand almost better than any other people the art of properly roasting a joint', although his observation that the art of cooking in England didn't extend much beyond roast beef and plum pudding somewhat undermined the compliment.

Spit-roast meat didn't taste of smoke: it cooked in front of the fire, not over it. Fat dripped into a pan set below, with no possibility of overheating. Trying to re-create the flavour of the past is difficult, but experiments give excellent results: succulent, cleanly flavoured, with crisp coatings. Managing the fire correctly, knowing how to spit a joint so that the weight was evenly distributed around it and how close to put the meat to the fire were all special skills. As a cook, one had to know how to prepare, or dress, and present all sorts of roasts; as a guest, to be able to carve was a desirable social skill. Leftovers were expected and were part of the domestic economy of large households.

A major difference between then and now is that we cook meat in an oven. Technically, this is baking, but it is now the accepted method for roasting. The change to oven roasting began after the coal-fired kitchen range was invented in the 1790s; gas and electric ovens followed in the 19th century. To people accustomed to spit-roast meat, the change was significant and not for the better. In an oven, meat effectively fries in the hot fat that drips from it, and escaping juices make the fat spit, splashing it on to the sides of the tin, where it burns. The texture of oven-cooked roasts is also different: closer and drier.

Seasonings and accompaniments for roasts have changed over the centuries, from medieval combinations of spices, through tastes for citrus and anchovies, and rich meaty concoctions to the 'plain cookery' of the late 19th century; our adoption of Mediterranean and Asian flavours is another link in this chain. Some items that have shown remarkable persistence are bread sauce, mustard, apple sauce, sage and onion, and redcurrant jelly, all established in the way that we use them today by the 18th century. We look for potatoes to accompany our roasts, but until the end of that century our ancestors would have expected pudding, perhaps a spherical, breadcrumb-and-flour plum one, or a batter type, still with us as Yorkshire pudding.

Sourcing a Roast

The first rule of good roasting is to buy good meat. The British Isles and Ireland have long been recognised for producing excellent meat, especially beef and mutton, but many factors other than simply 'buying British' come under consideration – flavour, price, animal welfare, place of origin. A roast from a supermarket can produce a reasonable meal, but one from a butcher or sourced directly from a farmer is likely to give something much better. Some suppliers are expensive, but others may be cheaper than supermarkets, and a knowledgeable supplier is likely to be able to tell you more about the animals.

Meat lies at the end of the food chain and represents a concentrated and precious food resource. The idea that it should be cheap is erroneous, and on balance it is better to pay a bit more for something well produced and to eat a bit less.

Intensive systems do not automatically equate with poor animal welfare but for really good flavour, a traditional slow-growing animal is likely to provide better meat. Animal welfare systems have been the subject of much debate over the past 30 years, and several assurance schemes exist to provide the consumer with some idea of how the food on their plate has been produced. There are four principal schemes, all voluntary, and each with a slightly different emphasis:

- Assured Food Standards ('Red Tractor') – established by the National Farmers Union, it covers many foodstuffs, including meat production in conventional intensive systems.
- RSPCA Freedom Food – specifically targeted at higher-than-standard animal welfare. RSPCA is the minimum welfare standard that the NT will accept from its tenant farmers and when sourcing meat for its restaurants.

- LEAF (Linking the Environment and Farming) – puts a greater emphasis on environmental responsibility.
- Soil Association – this organic certification relates to production systems, and the (non) use of herbicides, pesticides and medication.

All the schemes have their own assessment criteria, inspection systems and logos. Understanding their exact nature will guide you to some extent when choosing meat and other foods, but even within these there can be differences. Given that the producers who join them do so voluntarily, the chances are that they will be interested in well-produced food, but ethics and flavour do not necessarily overlap.

Most domestic animals and birds are from commercial stock bred for specific characteristics. Flavour is rarely top of the list – though leanness, fast growth, small bone structure and esoteric factors such as 'double-muscling' may be. Traditional British breeds of cattle, sheep and pig tend to be smaller, slower growing and have more capacity to gain fat than continental breeds, but slow growth can provide tastier meat and distinctive appearance adds locality and diversity to the landscape. Some breeds are considered 'rare', existing in limited numbers. There are several marketing schemes for their meat and, while eating something rare may seem odd, increasing demand for their meat helps ensure survival.

In conventional agriculture, maximum growth in minimum time is achieved partly by using specially bred animals. They tend to be reared on commercially produced concentrates made from a range of by-products whose composition depends on price. This applies especially to pigs and poultry, whose flesh can be dull and bland. It is less of an issue with beef, which is at least partially grass fed, and least of all with sheep, who graze pasture, moorland or saltmarsh. Farmers who take an interest in flavour often try to grow at least some of their own grain and other fodder crops for poultry, pigs and cattle. Feeding makes most difference to pigs and poultry, and as a general rule, any animal which has roamed freely will be more interesting on the plate.

Don't forget that meat, especially from cattle and sheep, has a strong link with our treasured landscape. Rainfall, temperature and topography are all well suited to grassland, and quite large areas that are unsuitable for growing crops will sustain cattle and sheep. The landscape includes many areas of distinctive flora, often partially created by grazing animals – cattle grazed on the rich lowland pastures of the Somerset Levels or the sweet grasses of the limestone uplands of West Yorkshire, or mutton from the Lake District fells or the short turf of the South Downs.

The age at which an animal is killed for meat also influences flavour. Most farmers don't want their stock lounging in field or shed eating expensive food after they have reached the optimum weight, so the majority comes from relatively young animals: lamb will be on the market at 4–5 months old, a pig at 3½–4 months. The BSE epidemic led to restrictions on the age at which beef cattle could be sold for meat, but they are now allowed to grow up to the age of 48 months (although the majority become meat at 30 months). Cattle breeds traditional to Britain score well for flavour, but take a long time to reach the weight at which they make good beef.

An important factor in the production of good meat is the treatment an animal receives at slaughter time, and how that meat is stored afterwards. Body chemistry means that an animal that is calm and rested when killed produces meat that keeps better, cooks better and tastes better. Keeping is particularly important for beef, lamb, mutton and pork, which are allowed to 'hang' in controlled, cool conditions. This process – also called maturing, aging or conditioning – allows changes in the meat to take place, increasing flavour and tenderness. Sheep and pigs are hung for relatively short periods of time, around 1 week. Beef may be hung for anything between 10 days and 4 weeks, although it is rare to find it aged for so long now, as the process occupies valuable space and evaporation means that the meat loses weight, thus increasing the price to the consumer. If you can buy beef aged for 3–4 weeks, it should be very good.

Because of the time and space needed, and the potential for loss of weight during the maturing process, vacuum-packaging is often used by companies both large and small. It is claimed that meat undergoes something akin to the maturing process when vacuum-packed. Meat in vacuum packs is, of course, much easier to handle and store.

Where to Buy Meat

Who is likely to sell good meat for roasting? To some extent, finding a good supplier needs trial and error. When buying from a supermarket, look for premium lines that are sourced from specified areas, breeds, groups of farms, or which are given some kind of special treatment (such as proper hanging). Read the labels. The price will almost certainly be a premium one as well. The more anonymous the meat is, the less likely it is to have been raised with care and treated with care. Some of the best meat producers work on a very small scale. To find meat for a good roast, the internet, local producer groups and food and drink festivals are all good sources of information.

One way to source good meat is to get it directly from the farmer who produced it. This has become easier in recent times: direct marketing schemes, farm shops and farmers' markets have educated consumers about some aspects of meat production and have also allowed them to ask, and sometimes to see, how the animals are reared. If you are lucky enough to find such a producer, you will increase your knowledge both of how meat is produced and treated, and may be introduced to suppliers of all sorts of other food.

Alternatively, try to find a butcher you trust, and then cultivate him or her. The Q Guild is an organisation of butchers whose members are committed to excellence. Good butchers will be able to provide much more than a slice of rump steak and a couple of chops. They should be able to prepare a joint neatly, deboning it if asked (then giving the bones to you along with the meat, of course); do any trimming and tying as necessary; and be able to provide extra beef or pork fat should the meat require it. They should stock breast of lamb and brisket for inexpensive weekday roasts. And they should have some knowledge of the food chain that has produced their meat. Most take great pride in the quality of the meat they sell, and specialise in meat from particular animal breeds or areas. Some have a close working relationship with the farmers who raise the meat, or they 'finish' sheep and cattle themselves, grazing them until they reach their specifications.

Game requires a special licence, which not all butchers hold; fishmongers may hold game licences. A farmers' market may be the best resort. Some specialist game dealers send items by post or courier, and these are the best bet for really unusual items such as snipe, woodcock or certain species of deer.

General Information on Cuts of Meat

When you have found a supplier, what should you buy? With a very few exceptions (such as a small rack of lamb), it is a waste of time to roast any piece of meat weighing less than 1kg (2¼lb). If the roast is just for two, then there will be leftovers, and there are plenty of dishes to make with those. As a very basic rule of thumb, allow about 125g (4½oz) per person for meat off the bone and 250g (9oz) per person for meat on the bone, but don't be too exact about this, especially if the meat is for an occasion when a really handsome piece will make the party extra-special, or if you want some leftovers for other dishes.

The most sought-after roasts are what are known as 'prime cuts', which have a large proportion of tender lean meat and little, or relatively little, connective tissue. They come mostly from the hindquarters of animals. There is a limited supply and a lot of demand, so they are expensive. Secondary cuts, such as shoulder of pork or shoulder of lamb or mutton, are quite fatty with complex muscle structure and more connective tissue; these still make good roasts, but they don't carve as elegantly. Beef brisket and breast of veal, lamb or mutton are well flavoured; they have a layered structure that can make them chewy, but still make good family meals. Belly pork, which might also be considered, is more tender and seems to be enjoying a revival of interest at present. In general terms, when buying fresh meat that is cut to order, look at the colour of the meat and the texture of the fat, and avoid meat with a lot of juice running from it, or that has an unpleasant smell.

Bones in meat help to conduct heat, so may shorten cooking times a little. They add flavour, especially to gravy and are very useful for making stock (see page 16), and can look impressive when the meat comes to the table. On the other hand, they make carving more complex, especially in joints such as shoulder of lamb or mutton. Joints such as rack of lamb and loin of pork should be chined – that is, part of the backbone removed – making them easier to carve. Most joints can be boned and rolled by the butcher on request (if you don't feel equal to the task), leaving a cavity suitable for stuffing. Take the bones home for the stockpot.

Fatty meat has been considered a public enemy by nutritionists for up to 40 years, and eating too much fat is certainly not a good idea. But leanness can be overdone too. A roasting joint needs fat; it is fat that gives much of the flavour to meat, and prevents it becoming dry during cooking. Some will be present in layers on the outside of the piece, or between individual muscles; 'marbling' will be visible as streaks and flecks of fat in the lean meat, especially in beef. If fat worries you, remember that some of it will cook out of the meat during roasting and can be skimmed off the juices and then discarded. Visible fat can be cut off your own portion, but don't expect everyone to follow your example.

Meat often arrives vacuum-packed, especially if it has come from a farmers' market or been sent by post. This does produce an odd smell on opening – not actively bad, but one that I would describe as dank and vaguely seaweedy. This can be minimised by opening the pack 1–2 hours before use. Discard any accumulated liquid, pat the meat dry with kitchen paper, put it on a plate and cover loosely with foil or a cloth, then leave it to breathe.

With all meat, take special notice of the 'use by' date if there is one, and keep it in the refrigerator or freezer as appropriate. Vacuum-packed meat can be frozen to extend its keeping time. Meat will keep well for relatively long periods of time in a deep freeze at a temperature of -18°C (0°F). It is important that frozen meat is properly thawed before cooking. Most pieces will thaw overnight at cool room temperature, although if the joint is very large, or the weather very cold, more time may be necessary. The process can be hastened a little by putting the meat in cold water (never warm) or with appropriate use of a microwave. Put the meat in a container large enough to catch the 'drip' – liquid produced as the meat thaws. Discard this and dry the surface of the meat before starting to cook.

Poultry and Game

Most poultry and game birds arrive swaddled in clingfilm. Remove the packaging as soon as possible, dry the bird with kitchen paper and pluck out any extraneous feathers. With game birds, the packaging makes it difficult to ascertain how cleanly they have been shot and how old they are – only young birds are suitable for roasting. The packaging also means you cannot smell them to tell how 'high' they are (see page 113). Try to find a butcher or game dealer who can be trusted to supply good-quality birds, unless you know a gamekeeper or go shooting and are prepared to dress the birds yourself.

Roasting Equipment

A sturdy tin, of the heaviest gauge metal you can afford, is essential, especially if you plan to roast meat on a regular basis. Tins come in a range of sizes, from small chop roasters to ones that will hold a medium-sized turkey. Use a tin just large enough to hold the pint comfortably, with a little space around it to allow for basting. If the tin is too large, the cooking juices will dry out and burn. A range of materials is also available: anodized aluminium is a good option if heavy steel is too expensive. A light, thin metal tin will do the job of containing the meat in the oven, but it will warp sooner or later – usually the moment you put it over heat to start making gravy. Once a tin has warped, the cooking juices will pool at one end and dry up and burn at the other, and it won't be much use. The oval, enamelled, lidded 'self-basting' tins, which everyone's granny has somewhere in the back of a kitchen cupboard, are fairly solid and big enough for most purposes. For chickens, and for slow-roasting and pot-roasting boned and rolled meat, a deep cast-iron pot with a lid is useful.

It is also useful to have a rack that fits inside a large tin, especially if you intend to roast ducks or geese. A two-pronged fork helps when manipulating hot roasts. A carving fork is fine for this.

String, both thin and medium-thick, a few skewers and tinfoil are necessities. You may also want to buy a larding needle and a trussing needle (see page 12), and perhaps a meat thermometer and one of the devices available for aiding removal of fat from gravy. A nice serving platter or a traditional meat plate look good at the table, but I find a board the best thing to carve on, especially for slicing boned and rolled joints. A carving knife and fork are essentials. The knife must be *sharp*, so you will need something to sharpen it with – a patent knife sharpener, a steel or a whetstone.

Preparing a Roast

Roasting has a specialist vocabulary and associated techniques, which add finesse to the results and are worth learning.

Barding and Larding

Very lean roasts benefit from extra fat added before cooking. The easier method is barding, which means covering the surface of the meat with thin slices of fat: bacon draped over the turkey breast is a good example. Bacon for barding needs to be unsmoked, streaked with fat and thinly cut. Pancetta is an option, particularly for small, quickly cooked items such as game birds. Slabs of beef or pork fat can be cut into thin sheets and used to encase lean cuts, or cut into strips and arranged over the meat in a crisscross pattern. The fat will need to be tied on to the meat with string before cooking.

Larding involves inserting lardons, or slivers of fat, into the meat at regular intervals. These melt during cooking and provide fat from the inside. Pork-back fat cut into narrow strips is the usual choice, but fat bacon can also be used. A joint can be larded by making incisions with a knife and inserting strips of fat into these (just as sprigs of rosemary and slivers of garlic are inserted into a leg of lamb), but a larding needle will give a better result. This has a hinged flap at the blunt end, which grasps one end of the fat so that it can be drawn into the meat and out of the other side.

If using a larding needle, remember that it is sharp. Some effort may be needed to draw the needle and fat through the meat. The needle may suddenly detach from the fat strip when this is achieved. Push the needle away from you, and don't let children play with it or stand near the work surface when you are larding meat. Larding can also be used for adding flavour. Roll the lardons in ground spices or finely chopped herbs, to carry flavour into the meat.

Trussing

Trussing isn't really necessary with oven roasting. The vestiges of this once quite complex skill can be seen in the elastic bands put round poultry. In the past, skewers or string were the norm. Trussing keeps meat, especially poultry and game birds, in a neat and tidy shape during cooking, drawing the wings and legs of the bird close to the body. I find that the legs cook more slowly than the breasts of trussed birds, and prefer to remove any strings towards the end of cooking. Discard elastic bands before starting to cook. Like larding needles, skewers and trussing needles are sharp and sometimes difficult to draw through the meat – so take care and keep children out of the way.

Marinating

A marinade can be as simple as a little olive oil and lemon juice with a couple of thyme sprigs, in which the meat is left for 1–2 hours, or an elaborate mixture of wine, herbs and vegetables in which the meat soaks for several days. With a few exceptions, very liquid marinades are probably not a good idea for roasting joints, because they leave the meat soggy, but rubbing the surface with flavourings such as ground spices can be effective. It is sometimes claimed that marinades with acid ingredients help to tenderise meat.

The effect is fairly superficial, but they do add flavour, and some marinades help to extend the shelf life of uncooked meat by a couple of days – useful in the past, before refrigeration.

Stuffing

Boned joints, poultry and game give the cook the opportunity to add a layer of stuffing or forcemeat (a forcemeat or *farce* is more elaborate and fine-textured). It is a technique that was fully exploited in previous centuries. Stuffing can add flavours and fat, provide contrasts in taste and colour, and make a roast go further. Old-fashioned stuffing recipes tend to be quite dense and heavy, but this was deliberate. A texture similar to that of the cooked meat was the aim, so that the two would cut neatly together. Stuffing had the effect of moistening the inside of a joint, the slowly melting internal fat spreading gradually and evenly through meat turning on a spit – an effect mostly lost in oven roasting. Several mixtures are given here, mostly relatively light and principally for flavouring. Bread-based stuffings should use stale bread – if it is fresh, partially dry it in a low oven. For a light-textured stuffing, tear the bread into small pieces rather than reducing it to fine crumbs, and bind with a little melted butter and stock or milk. For a traditional, dense texture, add beef suet (about a quarter of the weight of this to the weight of bread) and bind with 1–2 eggs. Always calculate the cooking time to include the weight of the stuffing. Alternatively, cook the stuffing separately, baked in a dish, or made into cakes or balls and fried.

Basting

Basting means moistening the meat as it cooks – usually by spooning over the juices and fat rendered during cooking, or extra butter, wine or other liquid. The general idea is to help keep the meat moist by returning to it some of the fat that cooks out during roasting and to add flavour. It is less necessary with oven roasting than it was with spit-roasting, but most meat will benefit from occasional basting. Basting is particularly useful for poultry and game birds, as it helps to develop a crisp and delicious finish to the skin.

Dredging and Frothing

These are methods for finishing a joint to give it a crisp surface. Dredging means adding a coating, usually of breadcrumbs (with or without flavourings), during the final stages of cooking.

Frothing means dusting plain flour over the meat a few minutes before the end of roasting. If done with a light hand, the veil of flour effectively fries in the fat on the surface of the meat, literally frothing in the process; this also helps give a crisp, tasty finish to the skin. Too much flour won't cook, and gives what Eliza Acton in the 19th century described as 'an objectionable raw taste'. Sometimes flour is rubbed over a joint at the start of roasting to help the fat crisp.

Pot Roasting

One more step removed from true roasting, this is a method for cooking in a covered container in which it fits closely, with flavouring vegetables and aromatics plus a little liquid over gentle heat – braising, in other words. It is useful for meat such as shoulder of venison, which tends to be dry and tough otherwise.

Resting

Meat cooked at a high temperature, or fast roasted, benefits from 'resting' after cooking. This means leaving it on a warmed serving platter, preferably covered, in a warm place (next to the cooker, or in the grill compartment) for about 20 minutes, or longer with large pieces of meat. It is especially recommended for beef. The texture of the meat evens out, making it better to eat. It also gives the cook oven space for Yorkshire puddings or to finish browning roast potatoes, and time to fiddle around making gravy, sauces or cooking vegetables at the last minute.

Ovens, Temperatures and Time

Getting to know your oven is important for producing a perfect roast. The quirks of individual ovens make it difficult to predict exact cooking times and temperatures. The all-round 'soaking' heat of Agas and similar stoves makes them very good for slow, even, thorough cooking. Electric ovens are generally even in temperature throughout, and manufacturers make claims about the efficiency of fan-assisted ones. Gas ovens can be blazing hot at the top and cooler at the bottom, meaning that items must be moved around on the shelves during cooking. If you lack confidence with a new oven, begin with something good-natured and relatively simple – a piece of slow-roast pork, or a boned shoulder of lamb – and eat it with new potatoes. There is no point getting hot and bothered over a huge and expensive sirloin of beef, Yorkshire pudding and roast potatoes.

As a rule, beef, lamb, mutton and game may be cooked to any stage between rare and well done, depending on taste, but pork and poultry should always be fully cooked. Joints of meat vary in weight and shape, and people vary in the extent to which they like meat cooked. Prime cuts can be cooked quickly at high temperatures, but lesser ones need longer roasting at lower temperatures. Roasting time for meat is often calculated by allowing a certain amount of time per pound of meat, multiplied by the weight of the joint; this rule of thumb was worked out about 150 years ago when imperial measurements were the norm, and to convert it to metric, one has to remember that 500g is roughly equivalent to 1lb. Times and temperatures given in the sections on individual meats and recipes are guides.

Meat Thermometers

One way to make sure a joint is cooked is to use a meat thermometer. Insert it into a thick part of the roast before it goes in the oven (make sure it's not touching any bones) and check the reading as cooking progresses. Probe thermometers are also available – these cannot be put in the oven, but can be used to take a reading of the internal temperature of the meat if it is removed from the oven. Again, avoid any bones when using these, and withdraw the probe fairly slowly.

Gravy

'Gravy,' wrote Alan Davidson in *The Oxford Companion to Food*, 'in the British Isles and areas culturally influenced by them, is ... well, gravy, a term fully comprehensible to those who use it, but something of a mystery to the rest of the world.' Possibly some of the confusion is due to changes in meaning of the word over the last three centuries. It has referred to both concentrated essences derived from cooking large amounts of meat with water and flavourings and the juices that appeared when slashing half-cooked meat on the spit and pressing it; finally, it came to mean a sauce based on the juices left in the roasting tin, or a mixture made with packaged powder and water.

There is a general perception, promoted by the manufacturers of convenience foods, that whatever else gravy is, it should be thick, chestnut brown and plentiful. This isn't always possible by the deglazing method given here, but surely it's better to have a small amount of juice with a really concentrated taste of the meat, than a lot of starch-thickened mixture without much flavour?

Most joints produce a certain amount of juice as they cook. Some of this usually browns on the base of the tin, producing delicious flavours – a process known to chemists as the Maillard reaction. These juices can be used to make excellent gravy. The general method is this: remove the meat to a serving platter, then pour any accumulated fat and liquid from the roasting tin into a bowl. The base of the tin will have patches of slightly sticky, well-browned juices on the base and round the edges. These are full of flavour and should not be allowed to go to waste.

Take a little meat stock (or water from cooking vegetables if the former is not available, or even plain water) and pour into the tin. Use a wooden spoon to scrape all the browned patches into the liquid; you may need to put the pan over a low heat. This process is known as deglazing. Once all the residues have been incorporated into the liquid, add it to the accumulated cooking juices. Skim off any fat, and use the liquid to make the gravy. Wine, cider or brandy can also be used to deglaze, but need to be cooked for a while to mellow the alcohol flavour. Bought stocks can be used although they may not be as good as a well-produced home-made stock.

Carving

Carving is not about simply cutting hunks off a joint. A good carver can make the meat go further, cut it so that it is more tender to eat, and ensure there are leftovers for another dish. Carving divides the meat, helps everyone to similar portions, or to the size of portion they want, retrieves and divides stuffing from the roast, and shares out limited amounts of desirable pieces – the well-roasted outside, the fat that is considered to taste the best, and the most desirable portions of lean meat.

Much of the ceremonial aspect of carving has been lost, which seems a little sad. After all, the meat on the platter probably represents quite an investment for the household in both time and money, as well as a treat for all those who are about to share it, so why not have a bit of ceremony?

Invest in a good set of carvers – that is, a carving knife and fork. The former should have a long, fairly narrow blade with a slightly flexible tip for cutting round bones, and be capable of taking a good edge. The latter will have two long tines, and should have a guard that can be raised to stop the knife blade slipping back up towards your hand. The fork is used for steadying the joint (try not to stab it deeply and make puncture marks); the knife, if properly sharp, will do most of the work.

When carving, bear in mind the direction of the grain of the meat (the muscle fibres) and, as much as possible, cut across it. Joints without bone, such as beef fillet or topside, are simple to carve, as are any joints that have been boned and rolled. With these, it is simply a case of slicing through the meat as if cutting through a Swiss roll (but in much thinner slices – chunky slices of roast are not especially pleasant to eat).

Leftovers

Faced with a leftover joint, one could just eat cold meat, but though that can be perfectly good, it is not always the point. For interest, the sake of appearance or for another hot meal, cooks need to be able to use the leftovers of a roast for another dish. A piece of meat is an investment and one should get the best out of it.

Leftovers need care and attention to make them good, just like any other cooking. The cook has to know how to overcome problems such as the potential dryness of cooked meat, diminution of flavour, and a strong chance that someone will have polished off all the gravy. Should there be gravy left, it is sometimes suggested that thin slices of meat can be carved and reheated in it for another 'roast', but this is not satisfactory: the flavour of the meat is never quite as nice, the texture hardens, and the taste is faintly institutional. If a latecomer to the meal insists on a plate of meat and gravy, then fine, but do make sure it is really hot before they eat it. Meat and sauces are favourite homes for food poisoning organisms – and that also goes for dishes made with cooked meat, like shepherd's pie. If leftover dishes are supposed to be hot, they should always be thoroughly hot.

A half-used roast destined for leftovers should be allowed to cool, then covered and stored in the refrigerator. Use the meat within a couple of days, either cold or by converting it to other dishes. For cold meat – in sandwiches or with salad – carve the meat neatly into thin slices. Irregularly shaped pieces can go into dishes where the meat is cut into chunks or minced; trim them of fat and gristle first (those can go in the stockpot). If you can't use cold meat within a short space of time, then wrap it and put it in the freezer. Gravy, too, should be refrigerated and used up within a couple of days or frozen.

Bones and Stock

Stock is useful for adding to gravy, sauces, soups and many other dishes. If a roast contained bones, use them to make stock (the bones can be frozen if you can't do this straightaway). Use a pot into which the bones fit neatly; I use either a two-handled stainless steel pan with a capacity of about 4 litres (7 pints), adequate for a chicken or bones from small to average-sized joints, or a large slow cooker. You will get more flavour if you break or chop the bones, though this may be difficult with stronger ones. Remove any garlic and strong herbs such as rosemary or sage, lemon, and the remains of any stuffing.

Add any scraps of cooked meat too small or dried out to be useful, skin or gristle from the leftover meat, juice or jelly accumulated under the roast, and leftover gravy for which you have no other purpose. Bones left on plates (for instance, from a chicken) are OK to add, as bacteria will not survive the lengthy cooking. Also add fresh flavourings, such as ½ onion (leave the papery skin on); 1 scrubbed carrot cut into chunks; the green part of 1 leek, well washed; a little celery; 1 tomato; 1 bay leaf; some parsley stalks; a few black peppercorns; and a couple of fresh thyme sprigs.

Don't mix bones from different animal species (except veal or pork bones, which have more neutral flavours and mix well with any others) and don't add salt. Cover with water, put the lid on the pan and bring to the boil. Turn the heat as low as possible and simmer very gently for about 2 hours, checking occasionally. Add boiling water if it seems to be evaporating fast. If you can, put the pan in a low oven, or use a slow cooker: the stock will be better.

At the end of cooking, strain the stock, discarding the debris. Flavour can be concentrated by fast boiling to reduce the stock. When you feel it's strong enough, allow to cool, then cover and refrigerate. Remove any fat. Stock is best used within 24 hours of making it in summer or 48 hours in winter. Alternatively, freeze it in convenient amounts for later use, such as in the gravy of the next appropriate roast.

American Equivalents

Dry measures

1 US cup	50g (2oz)	breadcrumbs
1 US cup	150g (5oz)	plain white flour
1 US cup	175g (6oz)	raisins; sultanas; dried apricots
1 US cup	200g (7oz)	rice

Liquid measures

⅛ US cup	30ml (1fl oz)	
¼ US cup	50ml (2fl oz)	
½ US cup	125ml (4fl oz)	
1 US cup	250ml (9fl oz)	
1¼ US cups	300ml (10fl oz)	
1¾ US cups	425ml (15fl oz)	
2 US cups	500ml (18fl oz)	
2½ US cups	600ml (20fl oz)	

Measures for fats

¼ stick	25g (1oz)	
1 stick (½ US cup)	100g (4oz)	

Unless otherwise stated, salted butter, plain white flour, ordinary table salt and granulated sugar can be used for these recipes. Try to use unwaxed oranges or lemons where zest or peel is required.

Beef and Veal

Beef has long stood for all things good about food in England, excellent in quality and abundant in supply. To celebrate extraordinary events, whole oxen were roasted as on the ice of the Thames during the Frost Fairs of the 17th and 18th centuries. On a domestic scale, a roast sirloin or rump of beef was considered the best of food. Privileged aristocrats and their French cooks had game and fancy dishes – but plain beef was the natural food of the upstanding Englishman.

The motif of roast beef appears again and again, in cartoons, prints, in the kitchen scenes depicted in recipe books, in menus real and imagined. Henri Misson in 1719 said of the English that 'two Dishes are their Dinners; a Pudding for instance, and a Piece of Roast Beef'. Later that century, the Norfolk parson James Woodforde was serving the same combination to his tenants for Christmas dinner. Roast beef and Yorkshire pudding is still an ideal Sunday dinner. The pudding might once have been a plum pudding, and now it's always Yorkshire – but the beef remains.

Before railways, the demand for beef was fed by cattle from Scotland, northern England and Wales, driven on foot to fatten in richer southern pastures, sold through the cattle fairs, such as Manningtree, and eventually reaching London. Further back than that, oxen were also important as draught animals, fattened for food only when pensioned off. Beef must have been deeper in flavour (and possibly tougher) than we are now accustomed to. It also appears to have been fatter, judging from some of the 18th-century depictions. During this century, agricultural improvers concentrated on selective breeding for meat or milk, producing beasts of great size. This was the genesis of 'traditional' British breeds that are still valued as meat animals – Beef Shorthorns, Herefords, Aberdeen Angus and others.

In the 19th century, beef – and meat generally – was given extra importance by the infant science of nutrition. Protein was emphasised, and for a while it was thought that all the 'goodness' of beef could be extracted in bouillon and beef tea. The idea was given a commercial push by manufacturers who reduced beef stock by boiling it to a pasty substance, which was packaged in tins – the origin of beef extract (still with us as Oxo and Bovril), and gravy mixes.

Traditional breeds remained the norm well into the 20th century. Many areas of the UK were recognised as producing excellent grass-fed beef – lowland Scotland, much of northern England and Northern Ireland, less hilly parts of Wales and the Welsh borders, parts of Sussex and Devon. These animals take a long time to reach the optimum weight for meat and are short in the back, so have relatively less of the prime meat used for roasts and steaks than continental breeds introduced in the 1960s. This was a disadvantage when tastes began to change in the late 1960s and nutritionists cautioned against large amounts of red meat and particularly its associated saturated fat. Beef also became more expensive and the BSE epidemic damaged the image of British beef.

Eliza Acton's observation in 1855 that ribs, sirloin and rump were the proper joints of beef for roasting still holds good. These all come from the back of the animal. Sirloin (from the French *sur*, meaning over or upon the loin) has always been prized. It was usually served as a plain roast, although a method known as hashing is described in 18th-century cookery books. When almost roasted, the layer of fat on top of the meat was raised, and the lean cut out except around the edges; the meat was finely minced with flavourings and replaced, the fat skewered back down. To us, this seems like an extravagant way of ruining a joint, but it was probably delicious. The long, tender 'undercut', located underneath the bones of a sirloin and better known to us as fillet steak, was usually left in place and carved with the rest of the joint, but sometimes it was removed, larded or stuffed and roasted or braised, a dish called 'mock hare'.

How the meat of the hindquarter – the rump – was divided in the past is less well known. There are plenty of instructions for roasting a rump or buttock of beef but it is not clear exactly what was meant. It was obviously a very large piece, weighing up to 7kg (15lb). How closely this coincided with the current definition of rump of beef and adjacent cuts such as topside, thick flank and silverside isn't known, but the chump end (which equates to the meat now used for rump steaks) was certainly used as a roast. Two rumps together with the sirloins, still joined together, made a baron of beef – a cut now unavailable, since BSE legislation requires all cattle to be split down the backbone and the spinal cord removed. Roasts from the forequarter have probably always been similar to those used now – rib roasts and sometimes brisket.

Attitudes to veal are more ambivalent than those towards beef. The fact that Britain has plenty of pastureland available all year round for keeping cattle may have encouraged a preference for beef, but veal was eaten as well. Pastureland is not infinite, and some calves (especially in areas that concentrated on cheese-making) have always been culled. Veal used to be a sought-after ingredient, especially in French-influenced *haute cuisine*. But over the years, and especially in the 20th century, welfare concerns were raised about the conditions in which veal calves were raised, demand fell and it can be difficult to buy today.

During the 18th and 19th centuries, veal cuts were close to the ones still used. Flank of veal was sometimes turned into a 'veal goose' by spreading it with sage and onion stuffing, after which it was roasted and served with brown gravy and apple sauce, 'a convenient mode of dressing the flank … for eaters who do not object to the somewhat coarse savour of the preparation', remarked Eliza Acton rather sniffily when quoting a 'City of London receipt'. It was usual to stuff veal and serve it with sharp sauces to counteract a tendency to dryness and the bland nature of the meat. The old quality marker of whiteness in the meat was partly cosmetic (for recipes where the pale meat provided a contrast to some other ingredient) and partly a desire for delicacy in flavour – though this could be taken to the point of blandness.

Buying Beef and Veal Cuts for Roasting

Roasting beef is as much about cooking good meat by the correct method for the cut, as about recipes. Excellent beef is best bought from a good butcher, who may be on the high street or might be working with a farmer or farm shop. The best comes from dedicated beef herds grazing on open pasture and will have been allowed to hang for a couple of weeks at least before reaching the butcher's slab. The lean of beef should be a good, deep red colour (not bright red) and lightly marbled – flecked with streaks of fat. The fat visible in layers over the meat should be creamy-white and crumbly in texture.

Veal is a by-product of the dairy industry; anyone who drinks milk or eats cheese, butter, yoghurt or ice cream should not object to eating this meat. Although milk-fed veal at 2½–3 months old is still considered the best, there is an alternative: this is 'rosy', or rosé, veal, which has a deep pink colour with only a light streaking of fat in between the muscles, and comes from older, loose-housed or outdoor-reared calves. Tracking it down takes persistence, and once you find it you may have to order roasting joints, as demand tends to be for escalopes (the form in which most people encounter veal in restaurants). A butcher who deals with the catering trade, or the internet, are the most likely sources.

What to Buy, and How Much

The British method of butchering beef and veal tends to run across major muscle groups, cutting through fat and bone (rather than dissecting muscles out, which tends to be the practice in continental Europe). In the past, the names for cuts varied quite a lot regionally, although they appear to be fairly standard now.

Sirloin is expensive, and if you want a piece from the rear end of the joint with the fillet still in place, you may have to order it: the joint is more profitable when divided into sirloin, fillet and T-bone steaks. Working forwards, the front part of the sirloin is also known as the wing rib, with a good eye of lean meat but no undercut. Attached to this is the forerib, with streaks and layers of fat in the 'tail', getting progressively less lean. These joints respond well to fast roasting at relatively high temperatures. Buy sirloin by weight, and rib joints by number of ribs, although they can be boned and rolled if desired (which makes them easier to carve, but less splendid at the table). A fillet, or a piece of one, will be expensive and is usually used for Beef Wellington (see page 25 for a very special sandwich using this cut). Brisket (boned and rolled) has an excellent flavour, but is highly variable in size and fat content, and tends towards toughness. Be guided by the butcher's opinion on this one, and treat it gently, with long, slow cooking. Working back from the sirloin, the next cut is the rump, now principally used for steaks; behind this, at the top of the hind leg, lies topside, a very lean piece of meat that makes a good slow roast; and next to it the silverside and a muscle known as the pope's eye, also possible roasting joints. These need to be slow roasted or pot roasted.

Veal cuts for roasting include the loin (equivalent of the sirloin in beef cattle) and, behind it in the animal, the chump end or fillet and topside; towards the head, the best end (equivalent to a beef rib roast) and shoulder; the breast can also be boned and rolled with stuffing. Veal is lean and tends to dry out so treat it gently and use a slow roast method with secondary cuts.

Storage and Preparation

The British have traditionally considered that any home-produced roasting beef is full of flavour and far too good to be 'messed around with' – i.e. marinated or otherwise flavoured before cooking – and that when cooked appropriately, the meat will also be sufficiently tender. As far as flavourings are concerned, beef fillet (less pronounced in flavour than many cuts) can benefit from short marinating with oil and herbs, and light spicing makes an interesting change with slow-roast cuts. Otherwise, restrict seasonings to salt and pepper, and possibly a little mustard powder mixed with plain flour and rubbed into the fat of a sirloin or rib roast before cooking. Very lean beef, such as topside, benefits from barding with extra fat (see page 12). Rib roasts are sometimes 'French trimmed' – the chine removed completely, and the thin layer of meat covering the ends of the ribs cut away and the ends of the bones scraped clean.

Veal has a delicate flavour that is easily overpowered by strong seasonings. Good contrasts are light, lemony notes; salted meat such as ham or bacon; the nutty flavours of some fortified wines; and a mild mustard of the Dijon type. Stuffings are a good idea with veal. Because it is from young animals without much fat, veal can be dry. To help prevent this, bard with pork fat or spread a little butter over it before cooking. If you can obtain some veal bones (even in relatively small quantities) and use them to make stock, these will enhance veal gravy and many other dishes.

Times and Temperatures

How 'done' should roast beef be? Some people hate well-done beef; others don't like to see pink in the middle. In the mid-20th century, well-done meat seems to have been the norm, but since the 1980s, chefs and cookery writers have shown a very definite preference for underdone meat generally. If you are intending to use some of the beef cold or for leftovers, it's better if it is kept slightly rare. Very lean cuts of beef, such as topside, are better if they are done on the rare side of medium, because they have little fat and tend to dry out during prolonged cooking. But really, it's a matter of taste.

There are two basic methods for roasting beef. The first is sometimes known as high-heat or fast roasting. For a fast roast, give the meat 20 minutes at 240°C, 475°F, Gas mark 9, then reduce the heat to 180°C, 350°F, Gas mark 4 and cook for the following times:

- Beef on the bone: 15 minutes per 500g (rare); 18–20 minutes per 500g (medium); 25 minutes per 500g (well done).
- Boneless beef: 12 minutes per 500g (rare); 13–15 minutes per 500g (medium); 20 minutes per 500g (well done).

The second method is slow roasting. Cook at 150°C, 300°F, Gas mark 2 for the entire time, allowing 20–25 minutes per 500g for rare to medium, and 30–35 minutes per 500g for well-done meat. I tend to cook pot roasts even more slowly, at 140°C, 275°F, Gas mark 1 and allow longer – up to 60 minutes per 500g.

Veal, because it tends to dryness, needs gentle heat. It should always be well done, but be careful not to overcook. Start it at 190°C, 375°F, Gas mark 5 for 15 minutes, then turn the heat down to 180°C, 350°F, Gas mark 4 and allow 25–30 minutes per 500g.

Roast Beef and Yorkshire Pudding

a piece of sirloin or rib roast, or wing
    rib or forerib
about 1 tablespoon plain flour
1 teaspoon mustard powder
about 300ml (10fl oz) beef stock
salt and pepper

FOR THE PUDDING
2 eggs, beaten
100g (4oz) plain flour, sifted
a pinch of salt
150ml (5fl oz) milk mixed with
    150ml (5fl oz) water
beef dripping from the roast

Serves 6

Take the beef out of the refrigerator about 1 hour before you want to start cooking it. Calculate the cooking time by the fast-roasting method (see page 21). Preheat the oven to 240°C, 475°F, Gas mark 9.

Season a little flour with the mustard powder, salt and pepper and rub it into the fat. Put the meat, bones downward, into a suitable roasting tin and roast for 15 minutes, then reduce the heat to 180°C, 350°F, Gas mark 4.

While the meat is roasting, prepare the pudding batter. Mix the eggs, flour and salt. Try to avoid creating lumps. Then use a whisk to blend in the milk and water, to make a batter with the consistency of thin cream. Alternatively, put the ingredients in the goblet of a hand-held blender and whizz together until smooth. Leave to stand.

After the beef has been removed from the oven to rest, turn up the heat to 220°C, 425°F, Gas mark 7. Add 1 generous tablespoon of dripping to the Yorkshire pudding tin and heat it in the oven until smoking hot. Pour in all but about 2 tablespoons of the batter (it should hiss spectacularly if the fat is at the right temperature), then return the pudding to the oven. Cook for about 30 minutes, until it is rumpled up like a blanket, well browned in patches and light and crisp in texture.

To make the gravy, take the tin the beef was roasted in and spoon off any excess fat. Deglaze, preferably with stock. Let this bubble, and then, off the heat, stir in the remainder of the Yorkshire pudding batter, and keep stirring until the mixture thickens (you may need to heat it gently to achieve this). Add a little more stock if necessary to achieve the desired consistency, then taste and adjust the seasoning.

There is a tradition that Yorkshire pudding should be cut into squares and eaten with gravy before the meat; but these days it is usually served on the side of the plate with everything else.

Slow Roast Topside

Slow roasting is a good method to use for lean joints such as topside, whose low fat content means they have a tendency to be dry.

beef topside, 1.5–2kg (3½lb–4½lb)
extra beef fat, cut in thin slices
    for barding (optional)

about 1 tablespoon plain flour
about 150ml (5fl oz) beef stock
salt and pepper

Serves 6

If you wish to bard the topside, arrange the fat in a layer over the meat and tie it on with string. Put the meat in a roasting tin that it fits reasonably well. Put in a low oven, 150°C, 300°F, Gas mark 2 (use the highest shelf in a gas oven) and allow 25 minutes per 500g for rare to medium rare meat, 30–35 minutes for well done. About two-thirds of the way through cooking, season the meat with salt.

When the meat is cooked to your taste, remove it from the tin to a hot dish. Snip the strings holding the fat in place and discard them and the remains of the fat (the fat should have cooked through, so you may find it crisp and delicious). Keep the meat warm. Pour the cooking juices out of the roasting tin into a bowl, then deglaze the tin with a little stock and add this to the juices. Skim them, returning 2–3 tablespoons of fat to the roasting tin; stir in a little flour and allow it to cook and brown gently. Stir in the juices, plus stock as necessary to make the gravy; taste and correct the seasoning, then serve.

Horseradish Sauce

Mustard and horseradish have both been served with roast beef since the 18th century, and probably long before. Commercial English mustard of the Colman's variety is very pungent, and certainly stronger than French mustard or the wholegrain mustards that became popular in the 1970s. Horseradish is also pungent, though much moderated by making it into sauce with cream.

4cm (1½in) piece of fresh horseradish
    root, cleaned and scraped

250ml (9fl oz) whipping cream
a little salt

Grate the horseradish, using the smallest holes on the grater. Whip the cream until fairly stiff. Mix with the horseradish and season with a little salt.

Crème fraîche can be used instead of fresh cream, but don't try to whip it.

Pot Roast Brisket of Beef

Brisket is not an elegant joint, but it has an excellent flavour. This recipe is based on 'To stew a Rump, or the fat end of a Brisket of Beef in the French Fashion', recorded by Robert May in The Accomplish't Cook *(1660).*

2kg (4½lb) piece of rolled brisket
1 tablespoon olive oil
a handful of shallots, peeled
1 garlic clove, peeled and sliced
1 scant tablespoon plain flour
200ml (7fl oz) red wine
about 150ml (5fl oz) beef
   stock (optional)
1 teaspoon salt

FOR THE MARINADE
2 teaspoons black peppercorns
2 blades of mace
6 cloves
fresh root ginger, about 1cm (½in)
   cube, peeled and finely grated
1 generous dessertspoon
   demerara sugar
1 garlic clove, peeled and crushed

Serves 6

To prepare the marinade, put the peppercorns, mace and cloves in a mortar and crush roughly. Stir in the ginger, sugar and garlic, then rub the beef with this mixture. Cover and leave overnight in a cool place or in the refrigerator.

To cook the meat, wipe the beef to remove most of the ground spices. Heat the oil in a casserole and cook the shallots and garlic briskly, stirring frequently, until they begin to brown slightly. Remove to a dish, then put the beef in the casserole and brown it all over. Then put the shallots and garlic around the meat, sprinkle over the flour and add the wine. It should cover the base of the casserole to a depth of about 2cm (¾in).

Fit a doubled sheet of greaseproof paper neatly across the top of the casserole, trimming so that it doesn't stick out and burn, then put the lid on over this. Cook very gently for 4 hours; this can be done on the lowest possible heat on top of the stove, or in a low oven at 140°C, 275°F, Gas mark 1. Check occasionally, especially if cooking on top of the stove, and add a little stock if necessary, as the gravy tends to reduce and catch; also, sprinkle the salt over the meat.

When cooked, remove the meat to a serving dish. Pour off the gravy and set it aside for a few minutes, then skim off the fat. You should be left with a glossy, deep brown, rich-tasting sauce, which can be thinned with a little stock or water if you like. Check the seasoning. Slice the meat thinly, and pass round the gravy and some mashed potatoes.

Right: Pot Roast Brisket of Beef.
Next page: Slow Roast Topside with Horseradish Sauce.

Shooter's Sandwich

*Whatever loaf you choose, it shouldn't be too slender, as the steak will 'shrink up'
and become wider during cooking.*

a piece of fillet steak from the 'tail'
    end, weighing about 500g (1lb 2oz)
2 tablespoons olive oil
100g (4oz) button mushrooms, sliced
15g (½oz) dried sliced porcini
    mushrooms (optional), soaked in
    100ml (3½fl oz) warm water for
    30 minutes – keep the soaking liquid
1 ciabatta loaf
salt

FOR THE MARINADE
4 tablespoons red wine
2 teaspoons balsamic vinegar
1 garlic clove, peeled and crushed
1 dessertspoon finely chopped parsley
1 bay leaf, shredded
3–4 thyme sprigs, leaves only
3–4 marjoram sprigs, leaves only, chopped
2 tablespoons olive oil
freshly ground black pepper

Serves 4

Mix the marinade ingredients and put them into a shallow dish or bowl. Add the piece of fillet, rubbing well with the mixture, and leave to marinate, turning from time to time, for a minimum of 2 hours. It can be left for as long as 24 hours. Preheat the oven to 230°C, 450°F, Gas mark 8.

Heat the oil in a frying pan or a small shallow cast-iron ovenproof dish. Add the sliced button mushrooms and fry briskly, stirring from time to time, until they begin to brown slightly at the edges. Stir in the soaked porcini and add their soaking liquid. If you have used a frying pan, transfer the mushroom mixture to an ovenproof dish at this point. Lift the beef out of the marinade, rubbing off any debris, and lay it on top of the mushrooms. Pour the marinade in underneath. Roast for 15–20 minutes. The meat should be rare to medium.

Slice the ciabatta in half lengthways and remove some of the crumb from each half, to leave a hollow into which the meat will fit. When the meat comes out of the oven, lay it in one side of the bread and distribute the mushroom mixture over it. The cooking liquid should have reduced to a few tablespoons (if it hasn't, reduce it by fast boiling). Pour the liquid over the meat and mushrooms. Season with a sprinkling of salt. Put on the top half of the loaf, pressing it down firmly to enclose the filling. Wrap firmly in foil, clingfilm or greaseproof paper. Put a small board on top and weight lightly with a couple of books or tins. Leave for 5–6 hours, then unwrap and cut across in slices at least 1cm (½in) thick.

Left: Shooter's Sandwich.
Previous page: Roast Veal with Sorrel Purée.

Roast Veal with Sorrel Purée

A traditional combination in English cookery, and lovely for a meal in late spring. Sorrel is not especially easy to obtain, but it is worth growing it or trying to buy some because it makes a delicious accompaniment for many things besides veal. The sorrel purée is a method rather than a recipe; the relative amounts of sorrel and cream are fairly flexible.

a piece of veal for roasting
    (topside, loin or chump)
    about 1.5–2kg (3½lb–4½lb)
30g (1oz) unsalted butter
1 scant teaspoon lemon zest
    (preferably unwaxed),
    finely grated
¼ teaspoon black peppercorns,
    coarsely ground

1 fresh bay leaf – discard the central
    spine, and shred the leaf finely

FOR THE SORREL PURÉE
15g (½oz) unsalted butter
100g (4oz) sorrel, washed and picked
    over – remove any tough stalks
150ml (5fl oz) double cream
salt and pepper

Serves 6

An hour or two before you want to cook the veal, soften the butter and mix in the lemon zest, pepper and bay leaf. Rub this mixture all over the meat and leave it, covered, in a cool place.

For cooking, select a roasting tin or casserole into which the meat will fit neatly, without too much space round the edges. Do not cover. Preheat the oven to 190°C, 375°F, Gas mark 5. Cook for 15–20 minutes, then reduce the heat to 180°C, 350°F, Gas mark 4 and continue to cook, basting with the cooking juices from time to time. Salt lightly towards the end of cooking, and allow to rest for about 15 minutes.

Just before serving, make the sorrel purée. Melt the butter in a saucepan. Put in the sorrel, still damp but not wringing wet from washing, then stir over gentle heat until it collapses. The colour will change from a vivid green to a less attractive grey-brown, but don't let this worry you. As soon as it is all cooked, remove from the heat. Pour the cream into a clean pan and bring to the boil. Add the sorrel and cook gently for 2 minutes; add seasoning to taste.

Carve the meat in thin slices and spoon some of the buttery cooking juices over each plate. Serve with new potatoes and the sorrel purée.

Veal with Orange and Verjuice

The original idea for this came from a book first published in France by an author known simply as La Varenne. Translated into English as The French Cook *(1653), it was an important text in the development of cookery techniques. This recipe uses verjuice, an ingredient now unusual in British cookery, although it was once ubiquitous. Technically, it is the juice of unripe apples or grapes, and it gives a pleasant fruity sourness without being overwhelming. A few winemakers now produce pasteurised bottled versions, which are probably a little sweeter than in the past. If you can't get verjuice, use a not-too-dry white wine in this recipe.*

a piece of veal topside, about
   1.5kg (3½lb)
40g (1½oz) unsalted butter, softened
about 200ml (7fl oz) stock, preferably
   veal or chicken
about 1 tablespoon plain flour
salt

FOR THE MARINADE
zest of 1 orange (preferably
   unwaxed), in thin strips
zest of ½ lemon (preferably
   unwaxed), in thin strips
6 tablespoons verjuice
freshly ground black pepper

Serves 6

For the marinade, mix the orange and lemon zests with the verjuice and a little freshly ground pepper. Turn the veal in this mixture and leave to marinate for 5–6 hours, or overnight.

When you want to cook the meat, remove it from the marinade and scrape any bits of zest back into the marinade mixture.

Spread the butter over the meat, add a little salt, and put the meat in a roasting tin into which it fits reasonably well. Strain in the liquid from the marinade. Cook at 190°C, 375°F, Gas mark 5 for 15 minutes, then reduce the heat to 180°C, 350°F, Gas mark 4 and allow 25–30 minutes per 500g, basting frequently and adding a little stock to the tin if the juices show signs of drying up. About 15 minutes before the end of cooking time, add the zest from the marinade to the roasting tin (do not add it any earlier, or it will burn and blacken).

When the meat is done, remove it to a warmed serving dish and allow to rest. Pour the juices from the tin into a bowl. Deglaze the tin with a little stock, then add this to the juices. Spoon off excess fat, returning about 1 tablespoon of the liquid to the roasting tin, and sprinkle in a little flour. Stir over a low heat until it browns slightly, then stir in the cooking juices to make gravy.

Leftovers

Beef is one of the nicest meats to eat cold. A slice or two of it, slightly underdone, with a salad of green leaves and some potato salad, is excellent as a lunch or light evening meal for a hot day. It also makes good sandwiches (see page 29). Several recipes developed for other meats are also suitable for cold beef including Shepherd's (or Cottage) Pie (see page 45), Hashed Meat (see page 62), rissoles (see page 64) and croquettes (see page 122).

Veal is less interesting when cold – the flavour becomes positively bland and the dryness is accentuated. British cookery has few solutions for what to do with the remains of a roast of veal. It can be used for American Salad Sandwiches (see page 79) and French Forcemeat for turkey (see page 88) as well as Eliza Acton's Veal Loaf (see page 33).

Bubble and Squeak

This can hardly be said to be a recipe: it is more a method for reheating various bits of leftover roast dinner. There are probably as many versions of bubble and squeak as there are people who make it. Originally a dish of fried cold beef and cabbage, potatoes appeared in recipes later in the 19th century (perhaps influenced by Irish colcannon) and other vegetables were sometimes added. In the mid-20th century, it was often served with sliced cold beef. Leftover cabbage and mashed potato, fried, remain the two vital ingredients. Aim for about half and half by volume of the two vegetables. The variety of cabbage may vary, but whatever is used, it must be well drained.

There are few rules in making bubble and squeak: the ingredients and their proportions depend to some extent on the contents of the larder. Adding fried onions or bits of fried bacon is entirely up to individual taste, as is the medium used for frying. Beef or pork fat left from a roast or bacon dripping are all good. Butter burns too easily to work well with a potato-based version. Avoid oil and fat from lamb or mutton.

Heat a frying pan and add a little fat – just enough to cover the base – and when hot add the bubble and squeak mixture. Allow this to cook until the underside is nicely browned and crisp, then turn with a spatula. Don't worry if the 'cake' breaks up (one that keeps its shape is worryingly reminiscent of industrially produced versions), but continue to cook gently. Turning the mixture more during cooking evaporates some of the moisture and consolidates the mixture, although you will get a certain amount of the browned crust mixed into it.

Serve on its own, with cold beef, or reheated gravy, or as part of a breakfast fry-up.

Cold Roast Beef Sandwiches

Cold roast beef makes some of the best sandwiches. Use good bread with a bit of texture to it
– I prefer a mixed wheat and rye loaf that has a fairly close crumb. Butter the bread lightly.
The filling can simply be beef, thinly sliced, seasoned lightly with salt and pepper, and a
smudge of mustard or horseradish. Or try something more elaborate:

8 slices of bread, lightly buttered
4 dessertspoons mayonnaise
Horseradish Sauce (see page 23), to taste
cold roast beef, sliced thinly
gherkins or preserved cucumbers with dill
salt and pepper

Serves 4

Lay out the pieces of bread destined to make the base of the sandwiches. Mix some mayonnaise
(about 1 dessertspoon per sandwich, if using slices from a standard loaf) with a little horseradish
to taste, and spread it over each slice. Distribute the beef over this, then season lightly, and add
a few slices of pickled cucumber to each one. Complete with the remaining slices of bread.

8 slices of bread, lightly buttered
4 dessertspoons mayonnaise
Dijon mustard, to taste
cold roast beef, sliced thinly
Crisp Fried Browned Onions (see page 155)
salt and pepper

Serves 4

Proceed as above, but mix a little mustard into the mayonnaise instead of horseradish,
and scatter the onions over the beef.

Miroton of Beef

A classic dish of French bourgeois cookery, very good with roast beef, especially if it's on the rare side. The 19th-century chef Alexis Soyer gave a recipe in his book The Modern Housewife *(1849).*

60g (2½oz) unsalted butter
2 large onions, peeled and sliced
2–3 tablespoons plain flour
2–3 tablespoons red wine vinegar or sherry
600ml (1 pint) light beef stock or wine
1 bay leaf
500g (1lb 2oz) cold roast beef, carved in thin slices –
    trim off any hard outer edges
75–100g (3–4oz) fresh breadcrumbs (optional)
salt and pepper
parsley, chopped (optional)

Serves 4

Melt the butter in a large frying pan. Add the onions and cook gently, stirring often, until very soft and yellow. This will take quite a long time (don't allow them to brown). Once they are thoroughly soft, gradually stir in the flour to make a roux (you may not need it all). Splash in the wine vinegar or sherry, and then stir in enough stock, bit by bit, to make a thin sauce. Add the bay leaf and simmer gently for about 30 minutes. Taste and adjust the seasoning.

Put half the sauce on the bottom of a shallow ovenproof dish. Spread the beef on top, then cover with the rest of the sauce. Cover with foil and put in a moderate oven, 180°C, 350°F, Gas mark 4, for about 30 minutes to heat the beef through thoroughly (if the beef is well done to begin with, give it another 30 minutes, otherwise it may be tough).

To make it more special, sprinkle the top with a layer of breadcrumbs and return, uncovered, to the oven until they are golden – about another 30 minutes. Garnish with chopped parsley, then serve.

Cold Beef, Hashed

The standard English method for re-presenting leftover beef (or any other meat) was to make it into a hash – cutting the meat up small, making a sauce to reheat it with, and adding flavourings as taste and imagination dictated. 'There is not any Thing in which the Cook may so much indulge her Fancy as in a Hash; for almost any Thing may be put into it' wrote Martha Bradley in 1756. This is Alexis Soyer's Hashed Beef Another Way, which works well with small amounts of beef to make a dish for one or two people.

15g (½oz) unsalted butter
1 tablespoon finely chopped onion
50g (2oz) sliced mushrooms (optional)
75–100g (3–4oz) cold roast beef, cut into small thin slices
1 dessertspoon plain flour mixed with a little salt and pepper
150ml (5fl oz) beef stock
1–2 pickled gherkins, sliced
some vinegar from the gherkins
1 teaspoon chopped parsley or tarragon (optional)
walnut ketchup, to taste (optional)
salt and pepper

Serves 1

Melt the butter in a frying pan. Add the onion and cook briskly, stirring frequently, until lightly browned. Add the mushrooms, if using.

Toss the slices of meat with the seasoned flour, then add them to the onion and turn them in the pan to warm through. Add the stock plus the gherkins and a little of their preserving vinegar (don't overdo this; you can always add a little more towards the end). Bring to a simmer, then taste and add more seasoning if desired. If using the chopped herbs or walnut ketchup, add these at the end as well.

Beef Ragù Made with Leftover Beef

A reasonable beef ragù (the type of sauce better known in English as Bolognese sauce) can be made with leftover roast beef. It won't be as good as one made with fresh beef, but provided it is made with care and good ingredients, it will be quite acceptable mixed through a bowl of pasta or used to stuff vegetables for baking, such as hollowed-out courgettes.

30g (1oz) unsalted butter
60g (2½oz) unsmoked pancetta or lean bacon, finely chopped
1 medium onion, peeled and finely chopped
1 small carrot, coarsely grated
1 celery stick, washed and finely chopped
2 large mushrooms, washed and finely chopped
2 garlic cloves, peeled and crushed
250g (9oz) cold roast beef, trimmed of fat,
    gristle and outside bits, and minced
150–200ml (5–7fl oz) red wine
100–150g (4–5oz) passata (bottled sieved tomatoes)
1 bay leaf (optional)
a pinch of dried thyme (optional)
a pinch of dried marjoram (optional)
scant 1 teaspoon salt
freshly ground black pepper

Serves 4–6

Melt the butter in a large frying pan or flameproof casserole and fry the pancetta until the fat is translucent. Add the onion and cook over low heat until it begins to soften. Add the carrot, celery, mushrooms and garlic and continue to cook, stirring from time to time, until the vegetables begin to soften and brown. Add the beef and stir in well, then pour in the wine and allow it to bubble. Stir in the passata and the herbs, if using, and finally season with the salt and grind in some pepper. Simmer very gently for about 1 hour. Taste and correct the seasoning.

Eliza Acton's Veal Loaf

Eliza Acton gave this recipe under the name of Bordyke veal cake (Bordyke was the street in Tonbridge where she lived). It is intended for fresh veal but works quite well with the remains of a roast and it makes a meatloaf like a close-textured, coarse pâté.

700g (1½lb) cold roast veal,
   free from bones, fat and gristle
225g (8oz) unsmoked streaky bacon
2 medium eggs, lightly beaten
zest of 1 lemon (preferably unwaxed)

a generous pinch of cayenne pepper
a pinch of grated nutmeg
¼ teaspoon ground mace
¼ teaspoon salt
unsalted butter, for greasing

Serves 6–8

Preheat the oven to 180°C, 350°F, Gas mark 4. Mince or chop the veal and bacon together thoroughly. Mix in the eggs, lemon zest and all the seasonings. Grease a round ovenproof dish and pack in the meat mixture. Cover the surface with foil or buttered greaseproof paper. Bake for 1–1¼ hours. Smaller amounts can be packed in individual ramekin dishes, which need about 25 minutes baking.

   Eat hot with a light tomato sauce, or cold with salad and new potatoes.

Beef and Vegetable Broth

1 litre (1¾ pints) good beef stock
¼ medium-sized turnip or swede,
   washed and peeled
1 leek, washed and trimmed
3 celery sticks, washed and trimmed

a few leaves of curly
   kale, washed
2 large carrots, washed,
   trimmed and peeled
salt and pepper

Serves 4

Put the stock in a pan (one that will go in the oven is a good idea, or use a slow cooker) and bring to the boil. While it heats, chop all the vegetables finely and add them to the pan. Stir in 1 teaspoon salt. Cover, and when it boils, transfer to a low oven or a slow cooker and leave to cook. It should be ready after about 1½ hours.

   The fresher the vegetables, the better the soup will be. Finely chopped celeriac or kohlrabi, or a tomato, skinned and chopped, are all good additions.

Lamb and Mutton

Lamb and mutton both refer to the meat of sheep, but there is an age distinction, and – unless you are a shepherd or a butcher – the terminology can be confusing. Alive, a sheep is considered a lamb from birth in the spring until the turn of the year. For the next 12 months, the animal becomes a hoggett, and after that it is a sheep.

As meat, lambs may be killed at about 10–12 weeks old for Easter, but most reach the market at between 5 and 12 months (still called lamb, and probably what 19th-century authors referred to as 'grass-fed lamb'). Then it enters a kind of culinary no man's land, when it is really mutton, but mutton that is too young to have acquired flavour or character (very little is available). After its second winter, the meat will taste more interesting, especially if grazed on some distinctive species-rich grassland or hill pasture. The full flavour develops at around three years old, but to be really good, according to judges in past centuries, the best mutton came from animals five or even six years old, and wethers – castrated rams – were thought to give the best meat.

Five-year old wether mutton was always difficult to obtain, and is impossible to buy these days. The market for wool (which gave live sheep added value) has declined, and keeping animals beyond the age at which they can first be sold is uneconomic because of the feed required. Mutton seems to have lost favour some time shortly after the end of World War II, and is only just starting to come back, slowly, into fashion. Our ancestors ate a lot of mutton, some of it very fatty and coarse, which is probably why the market for it declined when ample supplies of frozen New Zealand lamb became available.

Until the mid-19th century there was a certain amount of 'house lamb' production, indoor rearing of out-of-season young lambs. These animals, which had pale, tender flesh but not much flavour, were a luxury for Christmas, eaten young.

Lamb, in the sense in which we now understand it, is more seasonal than beef: it is usually born between January and May in the British Isles. We've completely lost sucking lamb, but new season's lamb is sought-after for Easter, when the home-bred item will just be coming on to the market (some farmers lamb around Christmas specifically to supply the Easter market). The bulk of it becomes available in the late spring and early summer, running through to September or October. This is the point when lowland animals are getting towards being hoggetts. As the autumn progresses, good mutton becomes a better option than overgrown lamb – if you can buy it.

Lamb and mutton, when it arrived before the roasting range in kitchens of the past, was, like beef, sometimes regarded as too good to be messed around with. The best mutton was simply roasted, as was young house lamb. A favourite combination in English cookery books during the 17th and 18th centuries was mutton with oysters – cheap and easily available, these were mixed into stuffings, rolled in spice and herb mixtures and used to lard the meat, or added to the sauce. The dish went out of fashion in the second half of the 19th century, when oyster beds around the British coast were ruined by pollution, disease and bad weather and the shellfish became an expensive luxury. Another dish involved hollowing out the lean meat from a partly roasted joint – in this case, from the inside of the leg – then chopping and pounding the meat with flavourings, and stuffing it back in the cavity and returning it to roast. The meat off a shoulder, roasted until almost done, was also sometimes taken off the bone, and the meat cut away from the inside and hashed (from the French *hacher*, to chop or mince). The bones and outer layer were grilled and served on top of the hash, a dish sometimes called Shoulder of Mutton in Epigram.

Other cuts included chine and saddle. Chine was two best ends and the backbone in between, and it seems to have gone out of favour by the end of the 18th century. A saddle was both the loins, with the chump part of the rump attached; sometimes the kidneys (located under the loin) were taken out, each wrapped in a 'tail' of fat from the rear end of the saddle, and skewered to it as decorative full stops. This joint was regarded as suitable for large formal parties, and it appears in the novels of John Galsworthy on the table at Forsyte family gatherings – symbolic, perhaps, of stuffy upper-middle class conservatism. Like a baron of beef, this particular joint has vanished into history because of legislation relating to the dressing of sheep for sale as meat. A saddle of lamb can still be purchased, though you might have to order it.

We tend to forget that lamb was much anticipated as a meat for the early summer, and considered to go best with summer vegetables – peas, new potatoes and small turnips. Mint sauce fitted in with this general summer scheme. In the 18th century, cucumber-based dishes were often served with mutton, while the 19th-century preference was for redcurrant jelly or onion sauce. Stuffing was sometimes used with meat from sheep, more to soak up fat than to add it.

British cookery has a persistent thread of serving lamb or mutton with flavours derived from the sea. Laverbread is one such example, as is samphire (plainly cooked, and served as a vegetable accompaniment, or cut into short lengths and stirred into the gravy). Fish flavours such as oysters or anchovy (much used in the late 17th and early 18th centuries) are also found in many recipes and go surprisingly well with the meat, more so if you can source a piece of saltmarsh-grazed meat.

During the second half of the 20th century, cookery writers began to introduce ideas from the peasant and country kitchens of southern Europe and the Middle East. Strong herb flavours and the use of fruit with lamb or mutton reappeared in English cookery after an absence of about four centuries. The idea of larding a leg of lamb with slivers of garlic and sprigs of rosemary, or concocting a rice and apricot stuffing, both come from this interest in Mediterranean traditions.

Buying Lamb and Mutton and Cuts for Roasting

Butchers often identify where their lamb comes from. Some areas have been awarded protected geographical names for their lamb, including Wales, Scotland and Shetland. As always, the ideal supplier will know the farmers who rear the animals and will be able to tell you about the produce.

Lamb should hang for 7–10 days. Mutton can hang for longer; 19th-century cooks considered that it should hang for as long as possible. Look for firm, dull red lean in lamb and dull brownish-red in mutton, with hard white fat and small bones. Excessive fat is to be avoided. Mutton can be difficult to buy, but a good butcher may be able to source it.

Sheep are cut into fore- and hindquarters. The hindquarter includes the leg (known in Scotland as the gigot, pronounced 'jiggot'), a favourite roasting joint that weighs 2–3.5kg (4½–7¾lb), depending on the breed and age of the animal. It is usually possible to buy a half leg, which means you have to choose between a round piece of lean meat, or a longer, slimmer shank end, with smaller muscles, but sweeter meat. The loin (which together with the leg makes a haunch) is also a good roasting joint, but since it is usually cut into chops, this has to be ordered. Equally, you are unlikely to be able to buy a haunch except by special request.

The forequarter includes the 'best end', sometimes known as a rack of lamb. This is a very good small roasting joint, with a neat appearance when nicely trimmed; make sure it is chined and that the long bones are divided at the joints to make it easy to separate them. The shoulder contains the bladebone and the long bone adjoining it, plus a knuckle. Bonier and fattier than leg, it is a good roasting joint with a sweeter flavour, and is cheaper. A whole shoulder will generally weigh 2–2.5kg (4½–5½lb), up to 3–3.5kg (6½–7¾lb) for mutton, but it is often sold cut diagonally in half. Finally, the breast – a cut taken from the ends of the ribs – can also be used for roasting. It tends to be chewy, as it contains thin sheets of muscle interspersed with connective tissue, and is also fatty, but has a good flavour and is very inexpensive.

As with beef, the question of rare or well done is really down to personal preference. For those who are undecided, leg and best end are probably both better cooked on the rare side, but shoulder benefits from being fully cooked – this will cook out some of the fat and crisp up the skin.

For individual recipes, I have given specific temperatures and approximate times, but if all you want is a plain roast joint of lamb or mutton, times and temperatures for fast roasting are similar to those for beef, although I would start it at a slightly lower temperature:

- For a fast roast, give the meat 20 minutes at 220°C, 425°F, Gas mark 7, then reduce the heat to 180°C, 350°F, Gas mark 4 and cook for the following times:
  Lamb or mutton on the bone: 15 minutes per 500g (rare); 18–20 minutes per 500g (medium); 25 minutes per 500g (well done).
  Boneless: 12 minutes per 500g (rare); 13–15 minutes per 500g (medium); 20 minutes per 500g (well done).
- For slow roasting, which works well with leg of mutton, cook at 150°C, 300°F, Gas mark 2 for the entire time, allowing 60 minutes per 500g.
- For breast of lamb or mutton, see recipe on page 41.

Roast Leg of Mutton with Anchovies and Orange Peel

3kg (6½lb) leg of mutton, bone in

1 tablespoon olive oil

2 large garlic cloves, peeled
    and each cut into 2–3 chunks

1 large shallot, peeled and quartered

1 bay leaf (optional)

some fresh marjoram sprigs (optional)

200ml (7fl oz) red wine

200ml (7fl oz) well-flavoured stock

2 tablespoons plain flour

freshly ground black pepper

½ teaspoon salt

FOR THE LARDING

8–10 anchovy fillets preserved
    in oil, drained

18–20 fresh rosemary sprigs,
    about 3cm (1¼in) long

1 large orange (preferably
    unwaxed)

Serves 8

To prepare the larding, cut the anchovy fillets into strips about 2cm (¾in) long and 5mm (¼in) wide. Pare the zest from the orange to make about 20–25 strips of zest, roughly the same size as the anchovy fillets. Keep the orange – you'll need the juice later.

Take the mutton and use a sharp knife to make parallel rows of small incisions, about 4cm (1½in) apart, from the broad end down to the shank. In the first row, put a rosemary sprig in each incision; in the second, pieces of anchovy; in the third row, slivers of orange zest. Repeat until the larding ingredients have been used up.

Put the olive oil in a roasting tin. Add the garlic and shallot, the bay leaf and the marjoram. Sit the meat on top of this and sprinkle with the salt (don't overdo this, because the anchovy adds salt as well). Cook at 170°C, 325°F. Gas mark 3 for about 2 hours, then pour the red wine and the juice of the orange into the roasting tin and return to roast for a further 1½ hours, by which time the juices should be running clear. Put the joint on a warmed plate, cover loosely with foil and leave to rest.

Pour the cooking juices into a bowl and reserve. Put the roasting tin over a low heat. Stir in half the stock, scraping the tin to incorporate all the browned cooking residue, and add this to the reserved juices. Return the tin to the heat and add 2–3 tablespoons of the fat from the meat. Stir the flour into the fat and allow it to brown lightly, but don't let it burn.

Skim the rest of the fat off the top of the cooking juices. Strain the juices into the tin, stirring all the time, and bring to the boil to make a lightly thickened gravy. Add the remainder of the stock, then taste and correct the seasoning if desired.

Shoulder of Mutton with or without Oysters

This recipe uses shoulder of lamb, or preferably mutton. I have suggested a boned one, seasoned inside, but a bone-in shoulder can be used if you wish, seasoned on the surface. The oysters will add a mild but not obviously fishy note. They will also double the price of the ingredients, so you may wish to omit them on those grounds. Remember that not everyone likes oysters or can tolerate them. Without them, this is still a good recipe, based on one suggested by Robert May in his book The Accomplish't Cook *(1660), a wonderful compendium of recipes.*

1 shoulder of mutton, 2–2.5kg
   (4¼–5½lb), boned weight
1 tablespoon finely chopped
   fresh marjoram
zest of 1 lemon (preferably
   unwaxed), grated
a pinch of freshly grated nutmeg

250ml (9fl oz) dry white wine
12 oysters (optional)
1 small shallot, peeled and
   finely chopped
1 tablespoon plain flour
stock or water, to taste
½ teaspoon salt

Serves 6

If the butcher has rolled and tied the meat, cut the string and unroll it to expose the inside. Scatter over the marjoram, lemon zest, a generous grating of nutmeg and the salt. Re-roll and tie firmly.

Preheat the oven to 220°C, 425°F, Gas mark 7. To calculate the cooking time, see page 36. Put the meat into a roasting tin and cook for about 30 minutes. Baste with the wine, sprinkle the surface of the meat with salt and reduce the heat to 180°C, 350°F, Gas mark 4. Continue to cook until done to your taste. Baste with the cooking juices at intervals.

When the meat is done, remove to a warmed serving plate and leave to rest. Pour all the roasting juices out of the tin into a bowl and allow the fat to rise; skim off as much as possible and reserve. Open the oysters. Strain their liquor through a sieve lined with kitchen paper to catch any bits of shell or sand, and reserve in a separate bowl.

Add about 2 tablespoons of the fat back to the roasting tin, heat gently and cook the chopped shallot in it until translucent. Add the flour and continue stirring and cooking until lightly browned. Stir in the roasting juices to make a smooth gravy. If using oysters, add their liquor at this point, stirring, and bring to a simmer. Just before serving, stir in the oysters and continue to cook gently for a few minutes. They must be thoroughly hot. Otherwise, proceed as for a conventional gravy, adding a little stock and adjusting the seasoning to taste.

Rack of Lamb with a Herb Crust

The rack, or best end of neck of lamb, consists of 6–8 cutlets, joined together, and must be chined. Often the ends of the bones are cleaned of all meat, and sometimes decorated with paper frills.

Two racks presented with the bones forming a crisscross formation are known as a guard of honour; three, curved and stitched together vertically so that the meat is inside and the bones radiate in a sunburst, is a crown roast, which was very fashionable during the 1970s.

A lone rack of lamb is a good joint for 2–3 people (although don't expect leftovers), and also one that is nice cold; the coating of breadcrumbs recalls 17th- and 18th-century 'dredges' of flavoured crumbs.

1 rack of lamb, trimmed

1 fresh rosemary sprig

30g (1oz) fresh white breadcrumbs

2 tablespoons chopped parsley

1 tablespoon chopped basil

1 garlic clove, peeled and crushed

½ teaspoon salt

Serves 2-3

Preheat the oven to 180°C, 350°F, Gas mark 4.

Remove the parchment-like skin covering the meat (a thin layer of fat should remain) and scrape the bones if the butcher hasn't done this for you. Put the lamb, bones down, in a small roasting tin or ovenproof dish, tucking the rosemary underneath. Roast for 30–40 minutes, depending on the size of the rack.

While the lamb cooks, mix the breadcrumbs, parsley, basil, garlic and salt. After the initial roasting, remove the meat from the oven and turn up the heat to 200°C, 400°F, Gas mark 6. Carefully spread the breadcrumb and herb mixture over the fat layer, pressing it down well. Roast for another 10 minutes.

This roast does not produce any gravy worth speaking of, so if you wish to serve it hot, good accompaniments are those which add moisture, such as Boulangère Potatoes (see page 149) or a dish of baked tomatoes.

Slow-roast Mutton and Salsa Verde

This recipe was originally created for Herdwick mutton; these sheep, born with black pelts that turn grey or rusty brown as they grow, have distinctive pale heads, small curved horns, and are principally found on the highest of the Lake District fells. Meat from other breeds will work equally well, although try to acquire mutton rather than lamb. Salsa verde, which includes both capers and mint, recalls the English traditions of caper sauce with mutton and mint sauce with lamb.

a whole leg of mutton, bone in
salt

FOR THE SALSA VERDE
a good handful each of fresh mint, parsley and basil
1 small garlic clove, peeled and crushed
2 tablespoons capers, rinsed of any salt or vinegar
   in which they have been preserved
2 tablespoons Dijon mustard
2 tablespoons red wine vinegar
8 tablespoons olive oil

Serves 6–8

Salt the meat lightly and cook in a very low oven, 140°C, 275°F, Gas mark 1, allowing 60 minutes per 500g.

To make the salsa verde, wash the herbs and pick off the leaves, discarding the stalks. Blend all the ingredients together, taste and season.

Carve the mutton and serve the sauce separately.

Right: Slow-roast Mutton and Salsa Verde.
Next page: Rack of Lamb with a Herb Crust.

Breast of Lamb Stuffed with Capers, Garlic and Herbs

Breast of lamb is something the Victorians would have described as being suitable for family meals. It needs slow cooking, moisture, and a highly flavoured stuffing to add interest and counteract the fattiness. In the past, standard English mixtures of bread with herbs and suet bound with eggs were favoured, but these are very dense to modern tastes. I suggest using a mixture with flavours borrowed from salsa verde (capers, herbs), which works well with this meat.

2 breasts of lamb, boned
40g (1½oz) unsalted butter
1 medium onion, peeled and
    finely chopped
2 garlic cloves, peeled and crushed
2 tablespoons salted capers, well
    rinsed and coarsely chopped
a little chopped fresh mint

3 tablespoons finely chopped
    fresh parsley
large tablespoon chopped fresh basil
zest of ½ lemon (preferably unwaxed),
    finely grated
150g (5oz) crustless day-old white
    bread, torn into small pieces
splash of stock or milk, to moisten

Serves 3–4

Breast of lamb is flattish and thin, with one straight edge cut from the forequarter, which may still contain the ends of the rib bones, unless the butcher has already removed them. If you have to do this yourself, run a knife in between the bones and the meat on the outside, then cut them away from the lesser covering inside and slip them out.

To make the stuffing, melt the butter over a low heat and fry the onion and garlic until softened. Stir in the capers, herbs, lemon zest and bread, and add enough stock or milk to moisten the bread.

Spread the meat out, skin side down. Put a layer of stuffing on top of each piece, then roll from the narrow end and tie at each end with string – firmly, but not so tight that all the stuffing oozes out.

Preheat the oven to 140°C, 275°F, Gas mark 1. Put the lamb in a shallow roasting tin and cook for 3–3½ hours, pouring off any fat that the meat renders. Then turn the oven up to 200°C, 400°F, Gas mark 6 and give it a further 15 minutes to crisp up.

It will not produce gravy, but a light tomato sauce goes well with the caper-flavoured stuffing. Alternatively, serve a salad dressed with vinaigrette on the side.

Left: Breast of Lamb Stuffed with Capers, Garlic and Herbs.
Previous page: Dried Apricot and Almond Stuffing.

Dried Apricot and Almond Stuffing

While lamb or mutton cooked on the bone scores best for flavour, it is not the easiest thing to carve. Both leg and shoulder are often boned, creating joints ideal for stuffing. This recipe uses a fruit and nut combination derived from Arab cookery.

Stuff the joint, then roll and tie with string. Or, if using a boned shoulder, tie it as a 'cushion' – in four, like a parcel – or as a 'melon' – manoeuvre the stuffed meat into a rough ball shape, then take a long piece of string and wrap it four times round the meat, crossing at the poles, giving the appearance of eight sections like a cantaloupe melon. Carve a rolled joint into slices, and a cushion or melon into sections.

40g (1½oz) unsalted butter
1 small onion, peeled and very finely chopped
50g (2oz) almonds, blanched and cut into slivers
150g (5oz) crustless day-old white bread,
    torn into small pieces
75g (3oz) dried apricots, soaked for a few hours,
    then drained and chopped roughly
zest of ½ lemon (preferably unwaxed), finely grated
a generous pinch of freshly grated nutmeg
50–100ml (2–3½fl oz) stock or milk
½ teaspoon salt
freshly ground black pepper

To stuff 1 small–medium shoulder or leg of lamb

Melt the butter in a small frying pan and sauté the onion gently until translucent. Toast the almonds lightly in the oven for 5–10 minutes; watch to make sure they don't burn. In a bowl, combine the onion, almonds, bread, apricots and lemon zest. Season with a generous grating of nutmeg, the salt and some pepper. Mix well and pour in just enough stock or milk to make the bread moist but not soggy.

Use to stuff the cavity left by boning the joint and roast. To calculate the cooking time, see page 36. Alternatively, make into small balls and bake in a lightly greased dish for about 20–30 minutes at 180°C, 350°F, Gas mark 4.

Laver Sauce

Laver, or laverbread, is Porphyra umbicalis *(or* nori *in Japanese). This seaweed, washed and cooked for a very long time to make a soft, greenish-black purée, is a traditional food of the south Wales coast. In the past, it was also collected from the Somerset and north Devon coast. It is difficult to buy away from south Wales, although a good fishmonger may be able to get some for you. It makes a good sauce for a plainly roast leg or shoulder of mutton or lamb, especially saltmarsh lamb.*

75g (3oz) unsalted butter
450g (1lb) prepared laverbread
juice of 1 Seville orange
salt and pepper

Serves 4

Melt the butter in a saucepan, add the laverbread and stir gently until hot. Squeeze in the orange juice. Taste and adjust the seasoning with a little salt and pepper if you consider it necessary.

If Seville oranges are unobtainable, use a mixture of lemon juice and sweet orange juice instead.

Mint Sauce

By the mid-20th century, mint sauce seemed to be the preferred accompaniment for lamb, combining two elements that go well with this meat – a strongly aromatic perfume and a sharp taste. Unfortunately, it was often badly made.

For mint sauce lovers, Eliza Acton's recipe of 3 heaped teaspoons of finely chopped young fresh mint, 2 heaped teaspoons of caster sugar and 6 teaspoons of 'the best vinegar' (try a good white wine one) is a good formula. Stir together until the sugar has dissolved.

Cucumber Chutney

Cold lamb and mutton need strongly flavoured accompaniments. Pickles and chutneys, especially fruity ones such as apple or apricot, are one possibility. Another is a fresh chutney of the type routinely made in Indian cookery. While not 'traditional' to English food, these were appreciated by colonial administrators living in India during the British Raj.

The original recipe was given in a book called Common-Sense Cookery *(1905). Its author, Colonel Kenney-Herbert, was an army officer in India who wrote several cookery books in the late 19th century. His book expresses a sense of military precision combined with exasperation at the ways of Indian cooks and a desire to keep a good, if possibly somewhat extravagant, table. The only green herbs he used were parsley and chives, where we, and probably the Indian original, would add green coriander – a flavour not popular among the Victorian English.*

Make this just before you want to eat it.

5cm (2in) length of cucumber

a pinch of granulated sugar

1 dessertspoon white wine vinegar

about 1 tablespoon finely chopped herbs – a combination of two
   or more of the following: chives, parsley, coriander, mint

a small piece of fresh hot green chilli pepper
   (or to taste), finely chopped

1 dessertspoon olive oil

salt and pepper

Serves 3–4

Peel the cucumber and cut in half crossways, then cut both pieces into slim julienne strips. Dissolve the sugar in the vinegar and pour over the cucumber. Stir in the chopped herbs, chilli pepper and olive oil. Season to taste.

Serve with slices of cold roast lamb or mutton and a salad of bitter leaves, lightly dressed with lemon juice and olive oil.

Leftovers

Shepherd's (or Cottage) Pie

This dish, a standard method for using up leftover roast lamb or mutton, seems to have first appeared in the 1870s, when mincing machines were developed. Cottage pie is the name usually given to a beef version. This is a basic recipe for either beef or lamb.

1 tablespoon fat from the roast, or oil

1 large onion, peeled and finely chopped

1 garlic clove, peeled and crushed

450–500g (1–1lb 2oz) cold roast meat (remove any skin, gristle, most of the fat and any bits of herbs left over from roasting)

300ml (10fl oz) leftover gravy, plus a little stock

about 1 tablespoon chopped parsley

salt and pepper

FOR THE TOPPING

1kg (2¼lb) floury potatoes

200ml (7fl oz) milk

30–40g (1–1½oz) unsalted butter

salt and pepper

Serves 4

Heat the fat in a large frying pan and add the onion and garlic. Let it cook gently without browning for 10–15 minutes. Chop the meat finely, or put it through a mincing machine (this produces a softer texture). Add the meat to the pan with the onions. Stir well and add the gravy, plus a little stock (or water) if the mixture seems dry. Taste for seasoning, adding salt and pepper as necessary, then add some chopped parsley. Lightly grease an ovenproof dish and pour in the meat mixture. For the topping, peel the potatoes, chop roughly and boil until just tender. Drain and mash with the milk, butter, salt and pepper.

Preheat the oven to 190°C, 375°F, Gas mark 5. Cover the meat with the mashed potato, roughening the surface with a fork. Brown in the oven for about 30 minutes, or leave to go cold and reheat (same temperature).

If you are cooking the beef version, Cottage Pie, try stirring 2–3 teaspoons of truffle oil into the mashed potato and sprinkle the top with grated cheese, such as strong Cheddar or Parmesan. Cook as above.

Pilaf

I first encountered the idea of a pilaf in Elizabeth David's Mediterranean Food *(1950),
although lamb and rice dishes appear in English cookery books as early as the 17th century.
It's a good method for stretching a small amount of leftover meat, or using up an odd slice
or two in a dish for one person. Ingredients and quantities depend to some extent on the
contents of the refrigerator and your appetite: the following are suggestions.*

75–100g (3–4oz) long grain rice
1 tablespoon pine nuts or blanched almonds, cut into slivers
1 tablespoon olive oil
¼–½ medium onion, peeled and chopped
1 garlic clove, peeled and sliced
75g (3oz) cooked mutton or lamb, cut into small chunks,
    with any skin, gristle and large pieces of fat removed
about 1 tablespoon raisins and currants, mixed
1 large ripe tomato, skinned and sliced, or 1–2 tablespoons
    passata (bottled sieved tomatoes)
salt and pepper

Serves 1

Boil the rice according to your favourite method.

Toast the nuts lightly in a heated frying pan, then set aside. Add the oil to the pan and fry the
onion gently. Add the garlic, and continue to cook until the onion is translucent. Add the meat, and
continue to fry gently. Add the raisins and currants, and keep stirring; after a moment, add the nuts.
Finally, stir in the tomato or passata.

By now, the rice should be cooked. Drain if necessary and stir in the meat mixture. Leave covered
for a few minutes, then serve with natural yoghurt or Cucumber Chutney (see page 44). Some Crisp
Fried Browned Onions (see page 155) make a good garnish, or add 1 tablespoon chopped parsley.

Pilaf Stuffing

To make a stuffing, use 200g (7oz) rice, and omit the meat and tomato. Use butter in place
of the oil, and add pine nuts, currants and chopped parsley to flavour, or almonds and apricots
(see page 42).

Scotch Broth

Stock from lamb or mutton bones has a distinctive flavour, best used with robust vegetable combinations found in the Scotch Broth tradition.

1 litre (1¾ pints) stock made with the bones from a lamb
   or mutton roast
40g (1½oz) split peas (yellow or green), soaked overnight
40g (1½oz) pearl barley
2 medium carrots carrot, scraped and sliced
small turnip, about 75g (3oz), peeled and chopped
1 leek, cleaned, trimmed and chopped
1 celery stick, washed and chopped
a few leaves of curly kale, washed and shredded
salt and pepper
chopped parsley

Serves 4

Put the stock in a pan and add the soaked split peas, barley and all the vegetables except the kale. Simmer gently until the peas and barley are soft. Add the kale and cook for about 10 minutes longer. Check the seasoning and add salt and pepper as needed.

   Divide the broth between bowls and add parsley just before serving.

Pork, Ham and Gammon

Pork comes from porkers. This may seem a statement of the obvious, but pigs are graded by age and weight. A porker is a relatively young pig, which has achieved the optimum weight for fresh meat but is not large enough for salting for bacon and ham (for that, one needs, naturally, a baconer). Pigs for fresh pork can be grown on to be older and heavier, but as with all animal rearing, the economics of feed versus the return on the meat come into play. In some cultures pork is taboo, but to the poor of the British Isles, and much of Europe, it often provided the small amount of meat they ate for most of the year. Pigs breed fast and have large litters, and a piglet could be acquired for relatively little money. In towns, they were fed on household scraps and what they could scavenge in the street (in spite of the authorities' attempts to control them, pigs were a common sight in the streets of many towns until the early 18th century).

In the countryside they might have been confined in a sty, or allowed a freer range (although pannage, the autumn feeding of pigs on acorns and beechmast in woodland, seems to have declined after the Middle Ages). They had their place, too, in the wider rural economy, especially in cheese-making areas, where they consumed the whey left over from this process. In short, these were useful animals, quick providers of meat in restricted space, for relatively little outlay.

This does not mean that the rural poor ate roast pork every Sunday. For a start, fresh pork was considered dangerous in summer, well into the 19th century. The meat does not keep well in hot weather, and effective refrigeration did not develop until the 1880s. Pigs were killed only during the cooler months of the year – the rule of thumb being only when there is an 'r' in the month (like oysters). In addition, most of the meat was salted for hams and bacon. These were stored and used slowly throughout the year, until the next pig was ready for the kill, although the hams were often sold to pay various household expenses, including the acquisition of the next piglet.

The fresh pork that the poor got under this system was usually the offcuts from baconers. The better-off, who could afford to buy meat, might acquire the cuts we are familiar with, but recipes for roasting pork in British culinary traditions are few and mostly simple. Favourite cuts seem to have been leg of pork and griskin – the lean part of the loin.

In the mid-19th century, Eliza Acton observed of roast pork that it 'is not at the present day much served at very good tables, particularly in this form', which may have reflected a general and longstanding feeling that it was not the most elegant of meats. She also commented on the 'old savoury stuffing of sage and onions', showing that this combination – still the one that springs most readily to mind when roast pork and English culinary traditions are mentioned – was considered a tradition even then.

Sucking pig was a different matter – special food. It was uneconomic to kill such a young and potentially productive animal for food (they were considered best at 3–4 weeks old). However, in communities whose ability to store fresh meat was limited but which had ready access to live animals, a sucking pig represented a luxury meal on the hoof. Given that a sow can have two or three litters a year, and breeds all year round, there was always likely to be one such pig available – and it could be cooked as soon as it was dressed (in 1756 Martha Bradley said it was best killed on the morning of the day it was to be cooked). Properly roasted, it provided an exquisite combination of tender, mildly flavoured meat with delicately crisp skin – and as with all relatively large and spectacular pieces of meat, it had extra status.

Roasting a sucking pig in front of an open fire required a great deal of attention to make sure the entire animal cooked evenly. They are long, and made even longer by the habit of trussing them with their front legs forward and hind legs back, thus requiring a fireplace that was also long. There was also the possibility that the plumper mid-section, closer to the fire than the slender little trotters, would be cooked through and scorching while the extremities were still raw. To counteract this, a special shield known as a pig-iron was sometimes suspended from the fire grate to lessen the heat received by the pig's midriff.

Of the meat that was salted, most bacon was used in the form of rashers to flavour other foods, and was enjoyed by both rich and poor. Hams, though, were a high-status item, which might be cooked whole to make an appearance on the tables of the wealthy. Usually they were boiled, but roasting and baking were alternative cooking methods, and were sometimes preferred to boiling. Both gammon and ham refer to the hind leg of a pig above the hock joint, cured by salting and drying, but there seems to have been a distinction in the past: a ham was cured as a separate piece of meat, whereas a gammon seems to have been left attached to a bacon flitch and cured as part of the side – a trickier process because of the varying thicknesses of meat involved. The words now seem to be used more or less interchangeably, although gammon sometimes implies a milder cure.

Buying Pork

Pork, like beef and lamb, has been bred for increasingly lean meat over the past 30–40 years. Pork that is very lean is dull in flavour and dry in texture. On the other hand, no one wants to pay for large amounts of fat. To produce really good pork, as with other meat, a balance has to be struck. Tradition – a breed that might have decorated the apple orchards of the south-west, or have been a talisman to a thrifty cottager – conflicts with the economics of bringing an animal to the optimum weight for meat in the shortest possible time with the highest proportion of lean and desirable prime meat. Pragmatism usually wins, and lean commercial stock is used for porkers that are killed for meat at about the age of 3½ months – but this will not be very flavoursome pork. Some butchers make a point of sourcing traditional and rare breed pork from slightly older animals, because the slower growth means more flavour. What the pig eats also makes a difference, both to flavour and to the texture of the fat.

Another factor in the flavour of pork is something called 'boar taint'. While male cattle and some sheep destined for meat are castrated, in Britain, male pigs are left intact, and this can lead to a distinctive flavour in the meat. Musky is a polite way to describe it. The issues behind this relate both to animal welfare and commercial implications to do with the way the animal gains weight. The theory is that taint will not be a problem since pigs are slaughtered for pork before puberty (this is when boar taint develops, as a result of hormonal changes). However, other factors operate: some pigs have more of the flavour, or enter puberty at a younger than average age, while some people are more sensitive to the flavour. The only way to counter this problem is to know your supplier, and to avoid the problem entirely you will either have to try and buy meat from female pigs, or find a supplier who castrates the males (which is important for traditional breeds that are grown on to be older than average).

When buying pork, look for lean meat that is pale pink, moist but firm; the fat should be white, firm but tender and present in reasonable but not excessive amounts. To store, remove shop wrappings, cover loosely and store on a plate or tray in the coolest part of the refrigerator.

Cuts for Roasting and Roasting Times

Because the lean is tender and the fat usually ample, most cuts of pork are suitable for roasting. The loin and leg contain the highest proportion of lean meat in large muscles. A whole leg of pork is a big joint that tends to be dry if not carefully cooked. Forequarter cuts tend to be fattier and have more connective tissue, but they still roast well, especially slowly. If it's crackling that you want, choose a piece of loin, a joint fairly even in shape along its entire length, with the skin lying in a gradually sloping sheet; it can produce spectacular results. Loin, as with other animals, has a long tender undercut (often sold separately as fillet); if you are fortunate, it will be left in place, an extra treat.

Most people would consider removing the skin to be a waste of a good joint, but if you want a result less fatty, or to marinate the meat, this really is a necessity. The skin on all pork joints should be scored, partly to help it crisp, but also to help divide it after cooking – most butchers will do this for you if asked.

Stuffing, including that old-fashioned mixture of sage and onion (see page 52 and 148) is sometimes used for flavour and to counteract dryness in cuts such as leg. Other flavourings for pork tend to fall into three categories, which may overlap to some extent: fruity, aromatic and sweet. In Britain, apple sauce or baked apples provide the former and are especially good with a really well-produced traditional-breed meat, the sweetness of the apple picking up on the inherent sweet note of well-fed pork. Lemon zest is also a good flavouring for pork, especially in combination with rosemary, thyme, fennel, garlic and black pepper. Chinese culture has provided a different range of flavourings, especially star anise, five-spice powder, and soy sauce in combinations with sugar or honey. These go particularly well with very slow roast pork. Traditionally the British have not marinated pork, but if you are using aromatic herbs, sprinkle them over the meat and rub in some time before roasting (even the night before).

Pork should always be thoroughly cooked. A rule of thumb for all cuts is to start the meat at 230°C, 450°F, Gas mark 8 for 20 minutes, then reduce the heat to 170°C, 325°F, Gas mark 3 and allow 25 minutes per 500g for prime cuts (leg, loin) or 30 minutes per 500g for other cuts. I prefer to cook belly pork and forequarter cuts on slow, 140°C, 275°F, Gas mark 1 for 60 minutes per 500g. A meat thermometer is especially useful when cooking ham or gammon. Because these are cured meats, they remain pink even when fully cooked, and it is less easy to tell when they are done.

Crackling

How to get crackling to crackle is, to some extent, a matter of knowing your oven and working out the optimum time and temperature for it. Slow roasting, is, in my experience, a more reliable way of producing crackling than fast roasting, simply because it gives the skin longer to crisp up and is less likely to scorch the edges of the joint. A method frequently recommended – at least since the 19th century – is to rub the skin of pork with olive oil and salt before cooking. Some people recommend basting; others don't.

Whatever method is used, three points help to provide good results. The first is that the meat must have a reasonable covering of fat: depending on the cut, I generally look for a layer of fat just over 1cm (½in) thick, and certainly not less. The next is that the skin should be properly scored; this needs to be done neatly in parallel lines at intervals of about 1cm (½in) apart, to about the same depth. The cuts might go down to the lean, but should not penetrate it. A good butcher will usually ask if the customer would like the skin to be scored. The third point is that the skin should be dry when the meat is put into the oven. This makes the following method, derived from Chinese cookery, seem rather strange, but it does work:

- Put the pork, skin side up, on a rack in the sink. Boil a kettleful of water and immediately pour the water evenly over the skin, allowing it to drain straight away. The skin will mostly dry quickly as the residual hot water evaporates, but blot it with kitchen paper or a clean cloth to make absolutely sure. Then salt and roast as normal.

If all else fails, the meat is cooked and the diners assembling but the crackling has failed to crisp up, free it – as an entire sheet – from the meat and leave the latter to rest. Put the crackling in a roasting tin or on a baking sheet with a lip and return it to a moderately hot oven, 200°C, 400°F, Gas mark 6, for 5–10 minutes. I use kitchen scissors to cut it into strips.

Roast Loin of Pork with Sage and Onion Puddings

a piece of pork loin, about
   2.5kg (5½lb)
150ml (5fl oz) dry white wine
generous 1 tablespoon plain flour
250ml (9fl oz) well-flavoured stock
   (pork, chicken or veal)
salt and pepper

FOR SAGE AND ONION PUDDINGS
fat (pork or beef dripping) for frying,
   plus some for the pudding tins
1 small onion, peeled and chopped
half the quantities of ingredients given
   for Yorkshire Pudding (see page 22)
12 sage leaves, chopped

Serves 6

Preheat the oven to 230°C, 450°F, Gas mark 8.

Prepare the pork for roasting, using your favourite method to encourage good crackling. Calculate the roasting time. Put the pork in a roasting tin and roast for 20 minutes, then reduce the heat to 170°C, 325°F, Gas mark 3. After about 1 hour, add the white wine to the roasting tin.

Meanwhile, prepare the sage and onion puddings. Melt the fat in a frying pan and cook the onion gently until translucent. Turn off the heat and allow to cool.

Cook the meat until done, checking from time to time. You may need to move it to a lower shelf in the oven to allow the puddings to cook on a high shelf; in any case, it should be removed from the oven and allowed to rest for at least 20 minutes before carving. Turn up the heat to 220°C, 425°F, Gas mark 7.

Make the Yorkshire pudding batter, then stir in the cooled onion and the chopped sage. Using a muffin tray or deep-holed bun tin, put 1 scant teaspoon of fat in each mould and then put into the oven to heat. When the fat is smoking hot, take the muffin tray out and divide the flavoured batter between the moulds, 1–2cm (½–¾in) deep in each mould. These puddings should be made a little thicker than Yorkshire puddings. Return the batter to the oven and cook for 15–20 minutes, or until puffed and golden, and done in the middle.

To make the gravy, pour all the fat and juices out of the roasting tin into a bowl. Set aside for a few minutes to allow the fat to rise, and then remove as much as possible to a separate container.

Put about 2 tablespoons of the fat back into the roasting tin and add the flour. Stir well over low heat, allowing the flour to cook and brown. Stir in the defatted juices, making sure you scrape up any residue clinging to the sides of the tin. Gradually add the stock (you may not need it all), stirring well, and bring to the boil. Season to taste.

Pork with Garlic and Herb Paste

The idea of cutting off the skin and putting a deeply flavoured paste under it before cooking came via a friend who used to test recipes and who remembered this idea with special fondness (thanks, Caroline). The seasonings suggested in this mixture are mostly ones associated with traditional pork sausages in Britain, with garlic, mint and lemon to give the mixture a lift. For an inexpensive roast, use belly pork, provided it is fairly thick and has a good layer of fat between the skin and lean. The original recipe used pork loin, and if you want to try this, follow the times and temperatures given on page 51.

a piece of belly pork, weighing
    about 2kg (4¼lb)
1 tablespoon each of fresh sage,
    rosemary and mint, finely chopped
8 garlic cloves, peeled and crushed
grated zest of 1 lemon (preferably
    unwaxed)
a good pinch of finely ground allspice

a good pinch of finely
    ground coriander
1–2 tablespoons olive oil
splash of white wine or stock
about 1 tablespoon plain flour
1 teaspoon salt
a generous grind of black
    pepper

Serves 4

Put the pork on a board and carefully cut through the fat layer between the skin and the meat (it helps if the pork is well chilled). Aim to leave just under 1cm (½in) fat attached to the skin, but don't worry too much if it is not possible. Keep the skin on one side and put the meat, bones down, in a roasting tin.

Mix all the ingredients except the white wine and flour to make a paste. Spread this evenly over the top of the meat. Put the skin back on top. Leave to marinate for 2–3 hours.

Preheat the oven to 140°C, 275°F, Gas mark 1 and put the pork in to cook. Allow at least 60 minutes per 500g, possibly a little longer. It will yield a lot of fat and some deep brown juices.

When the meat is cooked, remove it to a warmed plate. If the crackling hasn't crisped, put it in a shallow tin, turn the oven up to 200°C, 400°F, Gas mark 6 and return it to cook for 10–15 minutes, checking progress occasionally. Pour off all the fat and juices from the roasting tin into a bowl. Deglaze the tin with white wine or stock and add to the juices. Skim off the fat.

Put 2 tablespoons of fat back into the roasting tin and add a little flour, stirring with a wooden spoon over a low heat. Allow the flour to cook and brown a little, then stir in the cooking juices, and a little more stock if necessary, to produce gravy.

To serve, cut the meat in slices. This is best served with cabbage and plainly cooked potatoes – mashed, or small whole new ones.

Slow-roast Belly Pork with Root Vegetables and Oriental Flavourings

a piece of belly pork, weighing about
   1.5kg (3½lb), with the skin scored
2–3 large baking potatoes
1 large carrot
1 sweet potato
2 large parsnips
2–3 small white turnips, or about
   one-third of a larger yellow turnip
about 1 tablespoon oil or pork driping
6–8 garlic cloves, peeled but left whole
fresh root ginger, about 2cm (¾in),
   peeled and cut into long matchsticks
a few shallots, peeled and halved
   lengthways
salt

FOR THE ORIENTAL FLAVOURINGS
2–3 whole star anise
generous 1 teaspoon whole black
   peppercorns, lightly crushed
40g (1½oz) honey
2 tablespoons soy sauce
2 tablespoons dry sherry
200–300ml (7–10fl oz) well-flavoured
   chicken stock (keep about a
   third of this back for the end
   of cooking time)

Serves 4

Preheat the oven to 220°C, 425°F, Gas mark 7. Give the pork the boiling water treatment (see page 51), and salt lightly. Mix all the oriental flavourings in a small bowl. Wash, trim and peel all the root vegetables. Cut into chunks (turnip takes longer to cook and needs to be cut slightly smaller). Put them all in a pan, cover with cold water and bring to the boil for about 2 minutes. Drain thoroughly. Heat the oil in a roasting tin until very hot, add the vegetables and turn them until well coated. Mix in the garlic, ginger and shallots. Pour over the flavouring and put the pork on top, skin side up.

Roast for 15 minutes, then turn the heat down to 150°C, 300°F, Gas mark 2. The meat can now be left for 2–3 hours without attention, although you may wish to stir the vegetables once or twice.

About 30 minutes before you want to eat, turn the heat back up to 200°C, 400°F, Gas mark 6. Stir the vegetables, being careful not to break them, then return to the oven. Check every 10 minutes or so to make sure the crackling doesn't burn. When it is crisp, remove the meat to a warmed serving platter. Arrange the vegetables around it. Keep hot.

Skim as much fat as possible off the juices left in the roasting tin. Taste and add more salt if you consider it necessary, then pour the juices into a gravy boat. Use some hot chicken stock to thin them and to deglaze any cooking residue in the roasting tin, then add to the juices.

Loin of Pork Stuffed with Spinach

This roast of pork is inspired partly by an Italian recipe (grazie, Simone) and partly by the Lincolnshire tradition of stuffed chine (a section from the backbone of a pig and the meat either side, slashed and filled with large amounts of chopped green herbs). The preparation is quite elaborate, but it is easy to cook.

1kg (2¼lb) boned pork loin
a little lemon zest (preferably
    unwaxed), finely grated
1 tablespoon olive oil
salt and pepper

FOR THE SPINACH STUFFING
250g (9oz) spinach, any thick stems removed
50g (2oz) parsley, stems removed
¼ teaspoon salt
freshly ground black pepper

Serves 4

Buy a piece of pork loin with a good proportion of lean meat. Remove, or ask the butcher to cut away, the skin with the fat beneath, plus the 'tail' of fatty meat (use the latter in pâté or mince and add to a sauce for pasta). The lean meat remaining will have a thin white covering of sinew over one side. Work a sharp knife under one corner and separate it from the lean as neatly as possible.

Next you are aiming for a piece of meat that opens out like unfolding a leaflet. Place it so that the grain is at right angles to you. Take a sharp knife and make a cut into the left side, parallel to the grain and about one-third of the way down from the top. Don't cut all the way through – leave a 'hinge' at the right-hand side. Now start at the right-hand side and repeat the action, cutting about a third of the way up from the bottom, leaving the 'hinge' at the left.

This should give a piece of meat that opens out as a single sheet. Sandwich it between two large pieces of greaseproof paper and beat out with a rolling pin until it is roughly 1½–2 times larger, and about half the original thickness. Season the uppermost side with the lemon zest and salt and coarsely ground black pepper. Put the meat to one side while you make the stuffing.

Wash the spinach and pack into a saucepan. Cook over high heat for a couple of minutes, pushing it down and stirring until it has all wilted. Add the parsley and stir for a moment longer – just enough to soften it. Remove from the heat, pour into a sieve and press to get rid of the liquid. Put the mixture on to a board and chop coarsely. Season with the salt and a generous grind of pepper.

Take the meat and spread the spinach and parsley mixture over it, leaving about an inch all round. Roll up like a Swiss roll and tie firmly with string.

Preheat the oven to 200°C, 400°F, Gas mark 6. Put the olive oil in a small roasting tin, then add the meat and roast for about 50 minutes. Check occasionally to make sure the outside isn't cooking too fast, and season the outside with salt about halfway through cooking. To carve, simply cut in thin slices.

Pork Marinated to Taste like Wild Boar

2.5–3kg (5½–6½lb) leg of pork,
   boned and skinned
400ml (14fl oz) pork stock,
   or good chicken or veal stock
3 tablespoons plain flour
salt and pepper

FOR THE MARINADE
300ml (10fl oz) red wine
50ml (2fl oz) red wine vinegar
½ onion, peeled and sliced

2 shallots, peeled and sliced
2 garlic cloves, peeled and crushed
3 bay leaves, crushed
8–10 thyme sprigs
a few parsley stalks, roughly chopped
12 black peppercorns, bruised
12 juniper berries, bruised
3 cloves, bruised
zest of ½ orange (preferably unwaxed),
   cut in long strips
1 teaspoon salt

Serves 6–8

Put all the marinade ingredients in a saucepan and bring to the boil. Allow to cool.

Lightly score the fat of the meat in a diamond pattern. Put it in a deep bowl, and when the marinade is cool, pour over the meat. Turn it in the mixture, then cover and store in the refrigerator, where it can marinate for up to 4 days. Turn the meat in the marinade a couple of times each day.

When ready to cook, preheat the oven to 220°C, 425°F, Gas mark 7. Remove the meat from the marinade. Strain the marinade, reserving the liquid. Put the meat on a rack in a roasting tin and add a little water to the base of the tin. Cook for 20 minutes, then reduce the heat to 170°C, 325°F, Gas mark 3 for a further 2 hours, or until done. Baste with the reserved marinade at intervals and check that the liquid in the base of the roasting tin doesn't burn. If it shows signs of becoming too deep brown, add a little more water to the tin – the gravy is very rich but will burn easily.

When the meat is cooked, remove to a warm serving dish and allow it to rest. Pour all the fat and juices from the tin into a bowl, then deglaze the tin with a little of the stock and add this to the juices. The fat will rise to the surface – skim off as much as possible. Put about 3 tablespoons of the fat back into the tin and sprinkle in the flour. Stir well and allow to cook gently over low heat. Once it has turned a creamy colour, gradually stir in the reserved cooking juices, then the stock. Taste and check the seasoning before serving.

Right: Pork Marinated to Taste like Wild Boar.
Next page: Slow-roast Belly Pork with Root Vegetables and Oriental Flavourings.

Roast Ham or Gammon

When cooking ham, boiling is often thought of as the standard method, but opinions have always been split over this, and both spit-roasting and baking were also used. There are two basic ways to finish a ham, either by glazing or dredging with breadcrumbs, recalling 17th- and 18th-century spit roasts.

a piece of uncooked ham or gammon, without skin, weighing 2kg (4½lb)
a handful of cloves (optional)
a glaze or breadcrumb coating (see below and page 58)

Serves 8

Follow the supplier's instructions about whether or not to soak the ham. If the piece of meat is to be served glazed, score the fat in diamonds at about 2cm (¾in) intervals and stud with cloves.

Preheat the oven to 170°C, 325°F, Gas mark 3, then put the meat in a roasting tin and cover with foil. Bake for 30 minutes per 500g, and 30 minutes extra. For the last 30 minutes, remove the foil to allow the outside of the joint to brown, or use one of the finishes below.

Glaze for Ham

Where the idea of glazing the exterior of a ham with a shiny, sticky, sweetish finish came from is not clear. Possibly the glaze derives from the use of sweet wines for cooking ham, which seems to have been quite common in the 18th century. This glaze is based on a recipe from the 1930s American compendium, The Joy of Cooking. *The original called for bourbon, which works very well; a blended Scotch is fine.*

125ml (4fl oz) whisky, preferably without smoky character
125g (4½oz) Demerara sugar

zest of ½ orange (preferably unwaxed), cut in very thin strips
1 piece of star anise (optional)

Mix together all the ingredients, without dissolving the sugar. About 30 minutes before the end of cooking time, remove any covering from the meat and pour this mixture over it. If some of the sugar crystals remain on top, so much the better, because they will crisp a little during cooking. Use the mixture that runs into the tin and combines with the cooking juices to baste the meat at frequent intervals during the remaining cooking time.

Left: Roast Ham with Glaze.
Previous page: Loin of Pork Stuffed with Spinach.

Breadcrumb Coating for Ham

John Nott, in his Cook's and Confectioner's Dictionary *(1726), directs that a roasted gammon should be dredged with a mixture of breadcrumbs and finely chopped parsley. This produces a much subtler effect than the slightly alarming crust of cornflake-yellow crumbs now used on industrially produced ham.*

4 tablespoons breadcrumbs made from stale white bread
1 tablespoon very finely chopped parsley

The breadcrumbs are best made by putting a couple of slices of stale white bread in a low oven. Leave them until they are dried out and pale gold, then remove, cool and crush. The crumbs need to be quite fine: pulverise the bread in a food processor or beat it in a mortar to reduce it as much as possible. Then rub through a wire sieve to get the crumbs as fine as possible. Most will pass through to become near-powder. A few will remain in the sieve, but the process should reduce these to a degree of fineness that is acceptable, so use these too and mix in the parsley.

Put the mixture on a sheet of greaseproof paper. About 30 minutes before the end of cooking time, remove the foil from the meat and roll the side with the fat on over the crumb mixture, using the paper to help pat it over the surface. Return to the oven and cook for a further 30 minutes or until the coating is golden brown.

Roast Ham with Rhenish Wine

'Rhenish' wine (from the Rhineland vineyards) was much appreciated in Britain during the 17th and 18th centuries. Whether it had the same perfumed notes and degree of sweetness that it does today is not clear, but this recipe, after one given by John Thacker in 1758, is worth trying.

a piece of unsmoked ham weighing about 2–2.5kg (4¼–5½lb)
a handful of cloves (optional)
1 bottle light, medium sweet German wine, such as Niersteiner
scant 2 tablespoons plain flour
200ml (7fl oz) light stock
salt and pepper

Serves 6–8

Follow the supplier's instructions about whether or not to soak the ham.

When ready to cook, carefully remove the skin from the ham (try to leave most of the fat in place). If desired, score the fat and stud with cloves. Place the meat on a rack in a roasting tin and pour the wine in underneath.

Preheat the oven to 220°C, 425°F, Gas mark 7. Roast the meat for 30 minutes, then reduce the heat to 170°C, 325°F, Gas mark 3. Continue to cook, basting at frequent intervals with the wine. If this shows signs of drying up and catching, add a little water.

When the ham is done, remove to a warm serving plate to rest. Pour all the roasting juices into a bowl, allow the fat to rise and skim off as much as possible. Put about 2 tablespoons of the fat back in to the roasting tin and sprinkle in a little flour. Stir well, and allow to cook gently for a few minutes. Then gradually stir in the juices, scraping well with a wooden spoon to incorporate any residue from the base and sides of the roasting tin. Bring to the boil and stir in some stock to make a lightly thickened gravy. Check for seasoning: it is unlikely that much, if any, salt will be needed, but some pepper is a good addition. Also, if the meat has been cooked plainly, a couple of cloves crushed to powder can be added at this stage, to give just a hint of spice.

Serve with roast or mashed potatoes and greens.

Leftovers

British cookery traditions aren't strong on recipes for cold pork. The reasons are not obvious – perhaps it is to do with fresh pork being less ubiquitous than beef and mutton. Or perhaps it is simply that pork is pleasant to eat cold with salad and bread and needs little help. Certainly, pork is good with pickles and chutney of the old-fashioned type, especially mustardy ones like piccalilli, which cut the fat. Ham is another matter: it is more often eaten cold than hot. Ham salad has been a popular choice for a Sunday or other celebratory tea for 200 years, and the meat has probably been filling sandwiches for as long. Ham is also a useful ingredient in many other dishes, and can be used in combination with other meats in the following recipes: American Salad Sandwiches (see page 79), Chicken Sandwiches with Ravigote Butter (see page 80), Turkey Pie (see page 94) and Turkey Soup (see page 95).

'Fresh' Pea and Ham Soup

Stock from ham bones is traditionally used to make soup with dried peas – i.e., peas that have been stored for winter. There is nothing wrong with this and it can be very good; but we now tend to think of frozen rather than dried peas and these, too, make good soup – if a little different from the standard article.

1 litre (1¾ pints) well-flavoured ham stock
500g (1lb 2oz) frozen garden peas
a little cooked ham, cut in dice (optional)
salt and pepper
chopped fresh parsley or coriander, to garnish

Serves 4

Put the stock on to heat and add the peas. Bring to the boil and cook gently for about 10 minutes, then blend to a purée (this will have a slightly rough texture).

Return to the pan and reheat, seasoning with salt and pepper to taste. If you have any leftover ham, cut it in small dice and add these too. Serve with a little chopped parsley or coriander in each bowl.

Mustard Butter for Ham Sandwiches

The British – or at least, the English – have been making ham sandwiches for about 200 years, possibly longer. Mustard, usually of the pungent, bright yellow variety, was regarded as indispensable for these, at least for most of the 20th century. This is fine, but sometimes I prefer the Germanic tradition of mild, sweet mustard. Hence this flavoured butter.

60g (2½oz) unsalted butter, softened
20g (¾oz) mild Dijon mustard
20g (¾oz) soft light brown sugar
1 dessertspoon lemon juice

Makes 4–6 sandwiches

Mix all the ingredients together thoroughly. Taste, and add more mustard, sugar or lemon juice if desired. Spread on slices of good sourdough bread, and top with layers of ham, cut as thinly as possible.

Hashed Meat

about 500g (1lb 2oz) cold roast pork
   or other meat, thinly sliced

FOR THE MARINADE
2 tablespoons leftover gravy
   or concentrated stock
1 tablespoon red wine vinegar
1 tablespoon redcurrant jelly
½ teaspoon salt
½ teaspoon ground black pepper
a little pounded mace
rosemary and a little sage
1 small onion, peeled and sliced
   in thin rings
a few celery leaves, chopped
   (optional)
1 tablespoon chopped parsley
1 tablespoon red wine or Marsala

FOR THE BROTH
125g (4¼oz) onion, peeled
30g (1oz) celery
60g (2¼oz) carrots
60g (2¼oz) turnips
a small bunch of parsley
60g (2¼oz) good dripping
600ml (1 pint) stock or
   water, heated
the trimmings and any bones
   from the roast

FOR THE SAUCE
30g (1oz) unsalted butter
30g (1oz) plain flour
salt and pepper

Serves 4

For the marinade, put the gravy in a small pan with 4 tablespoons hot water, then add the remaining ingredients. Warm gently, and as soon as the jelly has melted, remove from the heat. Cool and pour over the meat. Leave for up to 24 hours.

For the broth, finely chop the vegetables and parsley. Melt the dripping and add all the vegetables. Fry briskly, stirring frequently until they begin to brown at the edges. Add the hot stock plus any trimmings, scraps of meat or bones from the roast. Simmer for about 1 hour with the lid of the pan ajar. Strain into a bowl, discarding the debris and allow to cool. Lift off the fat that rises to the surface.

Shortly before you want to serve the hash, make the sauce. Melt the butter in a pan and stir in the flour. Cook gently for a few minutes, then gradually stir in the broth and bring to a simmer, stirring for a few minutes to make a smooth sauce. Lift the meat out of the marinade. Strain the latter and add the liquid to the sauce, stirring well and returning to boiling point. Check the seasoning. Then turn the heat to low and lay in the slices of meat. Allow them to heat through, but don't let the mixture boil, or it will toughen the meat. Allow it to get thoroughly hot, and then serve.

Pork Rissoles with South-east Asian Spicing

Rissoles are really a kind of meatball, fried. It is known that medieval cooks used to make them, using pork. Our ancestors would have added whatever seasonings they considered pleasing or fashionable at the time: ginger, nutmeg, lemon zest, anchovy, Worcestershire sauce. If lemon grass had been available, they would probably have used it; there are fashions in flavours just as in most other things.

150g (5oz) cold roast
    pork, trimmed of skin,
    gristle and overcooked
    outside bits
50g (2oz) unsmoked bacon,
    without rind
2 mild green chilli peppers
    (or to taste), de-seeded
1 garlic clove, peeled

1 lemon grass stalk, washed and
    trimmed of its outer layer
a small handful of green coriander
    sprigs, washed
2 spring onions, washed, trimmed
    and finely sliced
1 egg
½ teaspoon salt
oil or fat, for shallow frying

Makes 18–20

Cut the cold pork and the bacon into rough chunks, put into a food processor and process to a mixture with the texture of coarse breadcrumbs.

Roughly chop the chillies, garlic and lemon grass, and whizz them in a blender, together with the coriander, to a coarse paste. Stir into the meat, then add the spring onions, salt and egg, and mix to a paste.

Heat a little oil in a frying pan and drop in generous teaspoonfuls of the mixture to make flat little cakes. Fry briskly for a couple of minutes, then turn and fry until both sides are golden brown. Drain on kitchen paper.

If you prefer not to fry the rissoles, they can be dropped on to a lightly greased baking sheet and cooked in the oven for about 10 minutes at 180°C, 350°F, Gas mark 4. Turn once halfway through cooking. Serve the rissoles with salad.

Flavourings
The flavouring amounts are suggestions; alter them to taste. Chillies can be very variable in strength. Lemon grass can be a bit tired and stale – but if it lacks zing, be careful about adding too much, as it also has a woody, resistant texture, which can be unpleasant.

Rissoles with Parmesan Pastry

Another recipe poached from Colonel Kenney-Herbert (see page 44). Worth taking pains over, these little deep-fried pastries make delicious morsels. The Edwardians might have eaten them at lunch, piled them up as a side dish for dinner, or used them to garnish some other dish; I like them as a nibble with drinks. The exact number of rissoles the recipe makes depends on how thin you roll the pastry and how you divide the filling. This is also good with beef.

250g (9oz) cold roast lean meat, trimmed of skin and gristle
leftover gravy (or use broth, see page 62)
salt and pepper

FOR THE PASTRY
100g (4oz) plain flour, plus extra for dusting
1 large egg, separated
50g (2oz) unsalted butter, softened
50g (2oz) Parmesan, finely grated
1–2 tablespoons water
vegetable oil, for deep frying

Makes 18–24

To make the pastry, put the flour in a bowl or on a slab, make a hollow and drop the egg yolk in. Add the butter and Parmesan and work together with your fingertips until it begins to form a paste. Add a little water and work together for a couple of minutes to make a smooth, soft dough. Cover and leave to rest while you prepare the filling.

Mince the cold meat finely; use a knife so that a little texture is retained. Mix with a few tablespoons of gravy to give a mixture that is moist but not runny. Add seasoning to taste – a little salt and pepper plus anything else that seems appropriate.

Dust a work surface with flour and roll the pastry out thinly (take care that it doesn't stick). For best results, it should be about the thickness of a twopence piece. Cut out circles with a diameter of 7cm (2¾in). Heap 1 generous teaspoon of filling on one side of each circle. Brush the edge of the pastry with a little egg white, then fold each circle of pastry in half to enclose the filling. Press the edges together gently to make shapes like tiny Cornish pasties, and give them a few minutes to firm up. Pastry trimmings can be pressed together and re-rolled to make more rissoles.

Heat the oil in a deep-fat fryer to 180°C, 350°F, Gas mark 4 and fry the rissoles until the pastry is golden brown. Remove with a slotted spoon, drain on kitchen paper and serve immediately. If you prefer, the rissoles can be baked for 10 minutes at 180°C, 350°F, Gas mark 4.

Right: Rissoles with Parmesan Pastry.

Potted Ham

A good method for using up cold ham. Potting started off with raw meat cooked specifically for the purpose (it was actually a means of preserving, on a similar principle to French confit d'oie). Over the years, the recipes changed and became lighter and softer (and eventually evolved into the various 'pastes' sold as sandwich fillings).

250g (9oz) cold cooked ham
freshly ground black pepper
ground mace, allspice or star anise
125g (4½oz) unsalted butter

Serves 4

Take a piece of cold ham and remove any gristly bits, skin and connective tissue, and any outside edges that have hardened and browned in cooking (these can all go in the stockpot). Fat (unless there is an excessive amount, which is unlikely these days) can be incorporated into the potting process. Cut the ham into small chunks and then blitz it in a food processor. Add some black pepper and your other chosen seasonings. Mace and allspice are traditional; star anise isn't, but a suspicion, finely pounded, is good. Don't overdo the seasoning, and if you choose to add star anise, don't mix it with any other spices but pepper, and add a very small pinch – otherwise, it will be overpowering.

    Beat the softened butter until creamy and mix in the seasoned ham. Put the mixture into a serving dish, such as a china soufflé dish, then chill. Serve for lunch or tea, with hot toast or good bread.

Left: Potted Ham.

Chicken, Guinea Fowl and Quail

Together with ducks and geese, these birds are classified as poultry – domestic birds reared for the table. With the exception of quail (which were always wild birds until the development of quail farming in the second half of the 20th century), these were small, adaptable, farmyard scavengers. They were often seasonal, and were sought after as delicacies at particular times of the year, but as domestic birds they had less status than game, and were more accessible to the general population. Chickens, especially, could be kept in very small spaces.

We buy chickens all year round, expecting them to be tender and varying in price according to weight, along with other factors relating to the way in which they are produced. Our ancestors priced chickens differently -- by age and time of year. In 1845, Eliza Acton wrote:

Fowls are always in season when they can be procured sufficiently young to be tender. About February they become dear and scarce; and small spring chickens are generally very expensive. As summer advances they decline in price.

This relates directly back to the cycle of egg-laying and hatching, which was at its lowest point in mid-winter, but increased dramatically as soon as the days began to lengthen. The majority of birds hatched around Easter flooded the market and the price came down as summer went on. They grew much more slowly than modern commercial stock – whose swift growth rate would have seemed extraordinary to farmers in the past.

A spring chicken really was a spring chicken – hatched in mid- to late winter, and ready for the table as a luxury in spring. It was simply roasted and appreciated for its tender flesh and delicate flavour. Smaller birds, the equivalent of poussins, were available, and were often grilled; older fowls were also plentiful, but were more suitable for boiling. Capons (castrated cockerels) were also once much esteemed, as they grew to be large, fat table birds.

Generally, we favoured young tender chickens -- and that is what we now get, but at the price of compromising production systems, with repercussions for the welfare of the live birds, and a loss of flavour. It is difficult now to imagine what a luxury a roast chicken was right up until the 1960s.

Domestic chickens have come a very long way from their probable origin as wild south-east Asian jungle fowl that were slowly domesticated and gradually spread westwards, arriving in the British Isles shortly before the Roman conquest. From then they scratched around farmyards, dunghills and urban backyards, probably with little change over the centuries – until, like all other farm animals, they began to receive the attention of agricultural improvers in the 18th and 19th centuries. They were improved by an input from Asian strains, which caused quite a stir because of their often very decorative appearance. The process by which the changes happened is largely unrecorded, because poultry breeding was generally a hobby for the urban working class, especially in the north of England. That said, many ladies – including Queen Victoria herself – kept fancy poultry as ornamental birds.

The counties around London, especially Surrey, Kent and Sussex, specialised in producing fat chickens for the London market, which showed a preference for white-fleshed birds. In the late 19th century, the creatures were crammed with oatmeal to give a fine flavour and texture. The ideal table fowl was required to have lots of tender white breast meat and light bones; economics, as always, looked for a bird that was early maturing. 'Sussex' breeds of hen developed from this demand, and the characteristics can still be detected in birds reared for the broiler system developed in the 1950s. The commercial breed used currently is the Ross Cobb, bred to gain weight as fast as possible and provide large amounts of white meat. In free-range systems with good feed it can produce a fine chicken, but doesn't show its best side when subjected to intensive broiler production.

At tables in the past, a plain roast chicken with bread sauce and some type of stuffing was considered fine material for a Sunday dinner, and in the 18th century was served as a delicacy as part of a larger meal of multiple dishes. The traditional accompaniment of bread sauce dates back to the Middle Ages, when breadcrumbs were used to thicken and bind spiced sauces, although it was often badly made, with a texture described by Colonel Kenney-Herbert as being 'like a bread poultice'. The use of other flavours and sauces with chicken followed the general trends over the centuries, but the British seem to have developed dishes using large amounts of pungent aromatics such as tarragon or garlic under French influence.

Chicken has many other advantages. Roast chicken is excellent cold, and was a good dish for a ball supper (especially with mayonnaise and salad), or for a picnic (an event much enjoyed by the English, despite the weather, and one that was a feature of 19th-century social life). The meat could be made into many other dishes, and the bones produce good stock – so they were always sought after. Somehow, despite the current unease about intensive systems for rearing chickens, the meat has never quite lost its image as a treat.

Guinea Fowl and Quail

Neither of these birds is related in any way to chickens, but both are farmed for their meat in Britain. They have white flesh and flavours that are in the same range as chicken. Sometimes they are classed with game – guinea fowl because it is gamier than chicken and shares the same tendencies as pheasant to dryness, and quail because in the past it was available only as a wild bird.

Guinea fowl are indigenous to Africa; known in parts of the Mediterranean by Classical times, they became more widespread in early modern times through links between Guinea and Portugal (hence the English name). The live birds have attractive spotted plumage and a rounded, bustling shape. They have been used in British cookery since the 16th century or before, but there are few specific recipes for them, and they were often treated like turkey.

As wild birds, European quail are often summer visitors to south-eastern Britain, but seem to be unobtainable unless you go out and shoot them yourself. They belong to the partridge family. The farmed birds are a domesticated variety, Japanese quail, which are usually very small and delicately flavoured. They are often treated in a similar manner to other small game birds in the English kitchen.

Buying, Storage and Preparation

As a child, I was privileged to live on a farm with ample opportunity to observe some (very) free-range hens. My favourite source now is a local farm shop run by a woman who takes enormous pride in her poultry flock, and an equal pride in their presentation – plump, properly plucked, nicely trussed, complete with giblets. The flavour is excellent. If buying in a supermarket, look at the quality symbols and aim for one that ensures the optimum in terms of space, access to outdoors and feed quality. The ability to range freely and a diet rich in grain both make a difference to the flavour.

Quality labels can help in making a choice. French Label Rouge birds should have been reared under excellent conditions with the best flavour in mind. They will be expensive. Supermarkets often have their own premium ranges, which make claims about welfare and feed. Individual producers (who mostly sell via their own shops and networks, or over the internet) often give a lot of detail about the conditions under which their birds are reared. Transparency in labelling, and in both supplier and producer, are all-important with chicken and poultry in general. The more anonymous a product, the less likely it is to have been treated with care at any stage.

Guinea fowl and quail also suffer from intensive rearing. It is difficult to know exactly what system has been used, generally you should assume this will have been intensive, unless stated otherwise. Both these birds are often imported, from unknown welfare systems abroad.

When buying chicken, a poussin is a very small young bird, weighing 450–500g (1lb–1lb 2oz), which will feed one person. A chicken – an older bird, though perhaps no more than 6–8 weeks old – will weigh around 1.5kg (3½lb) and feed 4 people. Older, larger birds – up to about 2.5kg (5½lb), and sometimes bigger – will feed up to 6 people. Guinea-fowl meat is similar to that of a good free-range chicken but is leaner and gamier in flavour. The birds are also smaller than chickens, and generally weigh 1–1.5kg (2¼lb–3½lb). One bird will serve 3–4 people. For quail, allow 1–2 birds per person.

The less a chicken costs, the more likely it is to need attention when it arrives in the kitchen. Remove and discard all wrappings and any elastic bands used to truss the bird (if it is trussed with string stitched through from side to side, the chances are that it has been properly prepared, and you won't need to do much). Pluck out any stubs and bits of feather. Dry the skin with kitchen paper, and dry the inside of the bird as well. Remove any obvious bits of pipe and trim the skin of the neck neatly.

Chickens, and most other birds, used to arrive with a little package of giblets – the neck, heart, gizzard and liver. Use these, if there are any, to make stock (see below). Very few chickens seem to come with giblets now. From the cook's point of view, this is not a good development.

The purpose of trussing a chicken is to make it look neat, compact and well shaped; to keep it tidy without any projecting bits to scorch (especially important for spit-roasting), ultimately giving a plump-looking bird which would present well at table. In practice, when roasting birds in the oven, I find that a trussed one tends to be undercooked between the thigh and the body when the rest of the bird is done. For this reason, I tend to remove ties about two-thirds of the way through cooking.

Chicken Giblet Stock

Should you manage to acquire a chicken with giblets, check the liver carefully to make sure the dark green gall bladder has been discarded. Add the liver to a stuffing mixture, pâté or a ragù for pasta.

Put the remaining giblets in a small pan with a bay leaf, a few parsley stalks and a few pieces of onion, carrot and celery if available, cover with water and bring to the boil. Skim, then cover and leave to simmer gently for about an hour. Top up with more water if necessary. Strain, discarding the debris and reserve the stock for gravy.

Roasting Times

Chicken must always be well cooked. Underdone, it is a notorious source of food poisoning. Because of this, it is also better not to stuff the body cavity of the bird, as the heat may not reach the centre of the stuffing by the time the meat is done. Cook the stuffing in a separate dish. Occasionally a thin layer of stuffing or some kind of flavouring is spread between the skin and the meat of the breast (see Roast Pullet with Gammon, page 73), a method which adds flavour and fat to the meat underneath.

Chicken, like turkey, is sometimes served with little sausages and bacon as well as bread sauce, or barded with bacon like game birds. If you don't bard it, protect the breast with buttered paper or tinfoil during the early stages of cooking.

Standard instructions for roasting a chicken are to start it off at 200°C, 400°F, Gas mark 6 for 20 minutes, then reduce the heat to 180°C, 350°F, Gas mark 4 and cook for 20–25 minutes per 500g until the juices run clear. Examine the meat between the leg and the body; if any hint of pink shows here, or in the juices which flow from the thickest part of the thigh when pierced with a skewer, the bird needs further cooking. Starting the bird on its side, then turning on to the other side, and finally on to its back during cooking helps to get it cooked evenly. Always allow for resting at the end of cooking time.

For guinea fowl and quail, see recipes on pages 74 and 76.

Basic Roast Chicken

½ lemon

1 chicken, weighing 2kg (4½lb)

a few sprigs of fresh herbs, such
   as parsley, thyme or marjoram
   (optional)

2 unsmoked bacon rashers (optional)

unsalted butter

3–4 tablespoons white wine
   or water

stock from the giblets (see page 69)
   or other chicken stock

scant 1 tablespoon plain flour

freshly ground black pepper

½ teaspoon salt

Serves 4–5

Preheat the oven to 200°C, 400°F, Gas mark 6. Put the lemon (which could be one you've squeezed all the juice out of) into the body cavity of the bird, along with the herbs. Bard the breast with bacon if you wish, or spread a little butter on it. Also spread a little butter over the roasting tin (just enough to stop the bird sticking as it starts to cook), and put the bird in. Calculate the roasting time.

It's often better to start roasting a chicken on its side, especially if it is a large bird and your oven is an unreliable gas one like mine. Cover with a lid if the tin has one, or with a piece of oiled or buttered foil. Roast for about 20 minutes, then reduce the heat to 180°C, 350°F, Gas mark 4. After another ten minutes, turn the bird on to the other side; cover and roast for another 15–20 minutes, then turn it on to its back. Add the white wine or water, cover and return to the oven for another 30 minutes.

Remove the foil, then baste the bird well with the cooking juices and sprinkle the salt over the skin. Return, uncovered, to the oven for the remainder of the roasting time. Check every 10 minutes or so to make sure the juices aren't burning (a good chestnut brown is OK; black definitely isn't). If they show signs of overcooking, add a little water. The skin should crisp and brown nicely. Baste once or twice more with the cooking juices – this helps to produce a really crisp, tasty skin.

The bird is done when the juices from the thickest part of the leg run clear (pierce it with a clean skewer or the tip of a sharp knife). Make sure the meat around the hip joint between the leg and the body is fully done; there should be no trace of pink. If there is, return the bird to the oven for a few minutes.

When it is fully cooked, remove it from the roasting tin to a warm serving plate while you make the gravy. Pour all the juices into a bowl, deglaze the tin with a little stock and add the result to the rest of the juices. Return the tin to the heat, then add a couple of tablespoons of the fat that will have risen to the top of the cooking juices and stir in the flour, allowing it to cook gently and turn a nutty brown. Remove as much fat as possible from the remaining juice and then stir gradually into the mixture in the roasting tin. Stir in the giblet stock, taste and adjust the seasoning.

Roast Chicken with Orange and Lemon

Citrus fruit were favourite flavourings for all sorts of meat dishes by the late 16th century, when they were used in combination with sweet spices and dried fruit. This recipe uses orange and lemon only, producing a very intense, slightly sharp-flavoured gravy.

1 chicken, weighing 2kg (4½lb)
juice and pared zest of 1 lemon (preferably unwaxed)
juice and pared zest of 1 orange (preferably unwaxed)
a few sprigs of fresh herbs, such as parsley, thyme or
    marjoram (optional)
splash of stock, to deglaze
salt and pepper

Serves 4–5

Start the chicken off as in the basic method (see page 70). When you turn the chicken on to its back, pour the fruit juices over. Cover again and return to the oven. About 30 minutes before the end of cooking time, uncover, baste, then salt the skin and add the zest, cut in thin strips, to the juices and return to the oven. Baste again a couple more times. Take special care to watch that the juices in the tin don't burn; add extra stock or water if necessary.

At the end of cooking time, the bird should have a deep gold-brown and very crisp skin. (Turn the oven up to 220°C, 425°F, Gas mark 7 for a few minutes to get it really brown and crisp at the end, if necessary, but do watch for burning.) There should be a relatively small amount of juice with a very concentrated flavour in the roasting tin. Pour off the juices and deglaze the tin with a little stock. Skim the fat off the juices and add the deglazed cooking residue, but don't attempt to make a thickened gravy – just give everyone a spoonful or two of the cooking juices with the meat.

Roast Chicken with Tarragon

The fresh, grassy, slightly aniseed note of tarragon is a classic partner for chicken in French cookery, with many variations on the theme, using poached or roast chicken, served hot or cold. Although recipes for the dish have appeared in several English cookery books over the last 100 years or so, it never seems to have become really popular, perhaps because French tarragon is not especially easy to grow in Britain (Russian tarragon, much more vigorous, lacks the flavour of the French variety). This is based on a recipe given by Elizabeth David in Summer Cooking *(1965).*

a small bunch of fresh tarragon
60g (2½oz) unsalted butter
1 chicken, weighing 2kg (4½lb)
1 teaspoon grated lemon zest (preferably unwaxed),
   plus ½ the lemon
100ml (3½fl oz) white wine or chicken stock
generous 1 teaspoon plain flour
150ml (5fl oz) single cream
salt and pepper

Serves 4–5

Pick the leaves off the tarragon and chop them. Mix a generous tablespoonful of chopped leaves with most of the butter – leave about 15g (½oz) for finishing the sauce. Put the tarragon butter, and the ½ lemon inside the bird. Roast as in the basic method given on page 70, basting from time to time with the cooking juices, turning it on to its back after 45 minutes and seasoning with salt and pepper towards the end of cooking.

When the bird is cooked, remove it to a warmed plate and pour all the juices into a bowl. Deglaze the tin with the white wine, making sure it bubbles fiercely, or with a little chicken stock. Add all the herby, buttery juices back into the roasting tin. Add the lemon zest and the remaining butter worked together with the flour. Stir well, then add the cream and the rest of the chopped tarragon and heat until the sauce boils and thickens.

Right: Roast Chicken with Tarragon.
Next page: Roast Chicken with Orange and Lemon.

Roast Pullet with Gammon

The original for this recipe came from John Nott in The Cook's and Confectioner's Dictionary *(1726). His recipes reflect the rich, meaty dishes popular among the aristocracy of the early 18th century. A pullet – a young laying hen – was an especially prodigal use of resources.*

100g (4oz) lean gammon (or unsmoked bacon, fat removed)
2 tablespoons finely chopped fresh herbs – a mixture of parsley,
    chives and basil
1 chicken, on the small side – about 1.5kg (3½lb)
olive oil or unsalted butter
splash of chicken stock, to deglaze
salt and pepper

Serves 4

Preheat the oven to 180°C, 350°F, Gas mark 4. Mince the gammon. In an 18th-century kitchen, some unfortunate maid or scullion would have had to do this on a board with two knives; for us, a food processor works very well. Mix the minced meat with the chopped herbs, then season; go easy on the salt, as the gammon will already be salty, but be fairly generous with the pepper.

Carefully ease the skin away from the flesh over the breast of the chicken. Divide the gammon and herb mixture in two and spread it over each side of the bird, between the meat of the breast and the skin. Pull the skin back and sew or skewer it at the neck so that the stuffing remains in place during cooking.

Spread a little olive oil or butter in a roasting tin and put the bird in. Cover the breast with a piece of tinfoil, as the skin cooks through quickly in this recipe. (Start the bird off breast down if this works better in your oven, but when you turn it on to its back, use a piece of tinfoil to protect the breast until cooking is nearly completed.) Calculate the cooking time (see page 69) and roast until the bird is three-quarters cooked. Then remove the foil, baste well, sprinkle the bird with salt and continue roasting until fully cooked.

Put the bird on a warmed platter to rest, removing any strings or skewers. Skim the fat off the cooking juices and deglaze with a little stock. Check the seasoning and serve.

Left: Roast Pullet with Gammon.
Previous page: Roast Guinea Fowl.

Roast Guinea Fowl

Recipes for roasting guinea fowl – or guinea-hens, as they were sometimes called – appear from the 19th century onwards; the English usually seem to have treated the birds simply, regarding them in the same light as pheasants. They can be tricky to cook well, as the meat on the breast tends to cook through and dry out before the legs are fully cooked. Starting the bird on its side for 15 minutes, then turning it on to the other side for another 15 minutes, before finally turning it on to its back overcomes this to some extent.

unsalted butter
2–4 rashers fat bacon
   (unsmoked streaky is best)
1 guinea fowl, about 1kg (2¼lb)

100ml (3½fl oz) port (optional)
150ml (5fl oz) well-flavoured
   chicken stock
salt and pepper

Serves 3–4

Lightly butter a small roasting tin in which the guinea fowl will fit nicely. Wrap the bacon around the breast of the bird and tie on with string.

Preheat the oven to 200°C, 400°F, Gas mark 6. Roast the bird for 20 minutes at this temperature, then reduce the heat to 180°C, 350°F, Gas mark 4 and cook for a further 25 minutes. Then remove the bacon, season with a little salt and continue to roast until the juices run clear. Allow to rest for about 10 minutes before serving.

To make the gravy, pour off all the cooking juices into a bowl and skim off and discard the fat that rises to the surface. Deglaze the roasting dish with the port, if used, or the chicken stock. Add the cooking juices and boil hard to produce a fairly small amount of thin, well-flavoured gravy. Adjust the seasoning with salt and pepper as necessary.

To accompany a guinea fowl, serve Bread Sauce (page 143) or Cashew Nut Sauce (page 75). A Wild Rice Pilaf is very good with this (page 75). A salad of watercress was favoured as an accompaniment by 19th-century cookery authors, but, writing in 1905, Colonel Kenney-Herbert suggested a salad of cos lettuce dressed with wine vinegar, oil, and a seasoning of 1 teaspoon each of chopped tarragon and chives.

Wild Rice Pilaf

20g (¾oz) dried chanterelles
125–150g (4½–5oz) wild rice
20g (¾oz) unsalted butter
1 medium onion, peeled and
    finely chopped
150–200g (5–7oz) chestnut mushrooms,
    washed, trimmed and sliced

50g (2oz) almonds, blanched
    and cut into slivers
1–2 tablespoons parsley,
    finely chopped
salt and pepper

Serves 3–4

Rinse the dried chanterelles and put in a small bowl; cover with boiling water and leave to soak. Put the wild rice in a pan and cover generously with boiling water; simmer gently until cooked, about 45 minutes.

Melt the butter in a large frying pan and cook the onion gently, stirring from time to time until the pieces begin to turn a pale gold. Add the chestnut mushrooms and continue to cook gently, stirring occasionally until all the liquid they exude has evaporated.

When the wild rice is cooked, drain and stir into the onion-mushroom mixture. Drain the chanterelles and add these too. Check the seasoning and adjust as necessary. Toast the almonds for 5–10 minutes. Stir these and the chopped parsley through the wild rice mixture just before serving.

Cashew Nut Sauce

40g (1½oz) unsalted butter
¼ small onion, peeled and very
    finely chopped
75g (3oz) raw cashew nuts

roux made with 15g (½oz) plain flour
    and 15g (½oz) unsalted butter
150ml (5fl oz) chicken or game stock
salt and pepper

Serves 3–4

Melt the butter in a small frying pan, add the onion and the cashew nuts and fry gently until the nuts become pale gold in colour. Empty the mixture into a food processor and whizz to a paste.

Use a small pan to make the roux, and once it is smooth and has cooked for a few minutes, stir in the nut paste plus enough stock to make a sauce. Season to taste and serve.

Roast Quail with Vine Leaves and Grapes

In the United Kingdom, quail are almost always farmed, and generally very small. They are best quite plainly cooked, and the standard instructions in English cookery books of previous centuries was always to wrap them in vine leaves. This is a nice conceit, if you can beg or steal some fresh leaves from someone, although I'm not convinced it makes a great difference to the flavour.

8 quail

a handful of small white seedless grapes

8 large vine leaves, if available

8 rashers unsmoked fat bacon, thinly cut,
   or unsmoked pancetta

unsalted butter, melted

100ml (3½fl oz) white wine

salt and pepper

Serves 4

Preheat the oven to 200°C, 400°F, Gas mark 6.

Season each bird with salt and pepper and pop a couple of grapes inside. Fold each bird in a vine leaf, then wrap a piece of bacon around it and tie in place with string. Brush each one with a little melted butter. Arrange the quail in a shallow roasting tin and pour over the white wine. Roast for 20–25 minutes, basting a couple of times with the wine and buttery juices.

Serve the quail still wrapped in their vine leaf parcels, with the cooking juices, skimmed of fat. Game Chips (see page 121) go well with quail, and a green salad tastes better with quail than cooked vegetables.

Leftovers

A good roast chicken is delicious cold as well as hot. Accompaniments can be very simple – some good bread, a well-made salad and a bottle of chilled white wine make it into a meal. Some more elaborate cold chicken dishes became classics of the English kitchen. Two are given below and on the following page, one from the late 19th century and the other devised for the coronation of Queen Elizabeth II. Although the recipes quoted are for whole chickens, they can easily be scaled down to cope with the remains of a bird already partly carved for a previous meal.

Julienne Soup

'Julienne' vegetables (cut into long narrow strips) were often used in soups in late 19th-century Britain. This is a typical mix, giving a light, fresh summery soup for a day when you have a well-flavoured chicken stock to use.

125g (4½oz) carrot
40g (1½oz) turnip
125g (4½oz) celery
200g (7oz) asparagus
125g (4½oz) onion, peeled
40g (1½oz) unsalted butter
about 1 teaspoon chopped
   fresh tarragon

1 litre (1¾ pints) well-flavoured
   chicken stock
1 small lettuce
½ teaspoon granulated sugar
salt, to taste
a little chopped fresh parsley
finely grated Parmesan,
   to serve

Serves 4

Cut the carrot, turnip, celery and asparagus stems into batons about 2cm (¾in) long and 5mm (¼in) square (the asparagus tips can be left whole and reserved until the end of cooking). Slice the onion into fine slivers.

    Melt the butter in a large saucepan. Add the vegetables and the tarragon, cover tightly, and cook over low heat for 15–20 minutes, stirring from time to time. Then add the chicken stock and simmer for about 10 minutes. At the end of this time, add the asparagus tips and the lettuce, cut into thin strips. Cook for 5–10 minutes longer. Add the sugar, and salt as you feel necessary. Ladle into soup bowls and garnish with chopped parsley. Serve the Parmesan cheese separately.

Mayonnaise of Fowl

This is the name Mrs de Salis gave in Sweets and Supper Dishes à la Mode *(1895).*
In typically late Victorian style, it was heavily decorated: she says 'garnish round the base
with a border of hard-boiled eggs cut in quarters, olives, fillets of anchovies, and chopped
aspic; ornament the top with a few sprigs of tarragon and chopped aspic.' Take this idea
as far as taste and the contents of the larder allow.

1 cold roast chicken
3 tablespoons olive oil
1 tablespoon wine vinegar
lettuce (use the inner leaves from soft, flat lettuces,
   or from cos, or little gem; or use lamb's lettuce)
mayonnaise
salt and pepper
sprigs of tarragon, chervil or parsley, to decorate

Serves 4–6

Joint the chicken by removing the legs and separating the drumsticks from the thighs. Cut off the wings and divide into joints (put the pinion in the stockpot, along with the skin of the bird). Cut the breast meat into neat pieces. Mix the oil with the vinegar, a little salt and pepper, and allow the chicken to marinate for 1–2 hours.

To assemble, make a bed of lettuce on a serving dish. Remove the chicken from the vinaigrette, allowing it to drain if necessary, and arrange on the lettuce. Use mayonnaise to mask the chicken and decorate with the herbs as desired. Serve immediately.

Variations

Mrs de Salis assumed that the cook would know how to produce mayonnaise of the right consistency. Out of expediency or nervousness about raw eggs, we'd probably reach for bottled mayonnaise, which is fine as long as it's a good one. Slack the consistency off with a little tepid water, or mix with a little plain yoghurt to give a runnier texture.

Aspic was a favourite garnish of 19th-century cooks, an item which would probably now be dispensed with, but a garnish of eggs, olives, anchovies and tarragon provides an excellent foil for the gentler flavours of the chicken and the mayonnaise.

Chicken Sandwiches

*Cold chicken makes a fine sandwich, alone, with salad, or in elaborate combinations.
The recipe below is based on one that appeared under the heading of 'American Salad
Sandwiches' in* The Cookery Book of Lady Clark of Tillypronie *(Tillypronie is a house
on Deeside, in Scotland). Lady Clark made a huge collection of recipes between 1841 and
her death in 1897. The correspondent who donated this one remarked that these were
'The only sandwiches which do not dry up at once in a journey in the United States'.*

100g (4oz) cooked chicken, free of skin, fat and gristle
100g (4oz) cooked tongue
4 tablespoons mayonnaise
celery salt, or table salt
a pinch of cayenne pepper
anchovy essence (optional)
6–8 lettuce leaves
tarragon vinegar
6–8 slices of good white bread

Makes enough for 3–4 sandwiches

Put the chicken, tongue and mayonnaise in a food processor and blend. Season with the celery salt
(remembering that the tongue may be quite salty), cayenne pepper and the anchovy essence, if using.

Dip the lettuce leaves in tarragon vinegar, and put one on a slice of bread; spread a layer
of the meat mixture over, and top with another lettuce leaf and another slice of bread.

I prefer this without the anchovy, and have to own up to having made it without dipping the
lettuce in tarragon vinegar. It still made good sandwiches. Lady Clark comments that the recipe
can also be used with ham and veal instead of chicken and tongue.

Chicken Sandwiches with Ravigote Butter

Another idea from Colonel Kenney-Herbert's Common-Sense Cookery *(1905), given in a short section on sandwiches. Ravigote butter is not something generally found in the modern kitchen, but it is delicious and useful for all sorts of sandwiches. The name is derived from the French verb* ravigoter, *to perk up.*

Burnet, a salad herb of long-established meadows, has pretty oval leaves with serrated edges. Its flavour is reminiscent of cucumbers. It is not usually seen on sale, but can easily be grown in a pot or a sunny corner. If it is unobtainable, either omit it, or replace it with parsley, which gives the classic French fines herbes *combination.*

This recipe makes quite a large amount but it can be frozen, or used with other dishes – with plain roast chicken or eggs, for instance.

The recipe works equally well with turkey or ham.

FOR THE RAVIGOTE BUTTER
30g (1oz) fresh chervil
30g (1oz) fresh tarragon
30g (1oz) fresh chives
30g (1oz) fresh burnet (optional)
250g (9oz) unsalted butter, softened

Makes enough for about 12 sandwiches

Pick over the herbs and wash them, then scald by placing in a small bowl and pouring boiling water over them. Leave for 2 minutes. Drain on kitchen paper, then put them in a blender and chop as finely as possible. Add the butter gradually, to achieve a paste that is as smooth as possible.

For sandwiches, take equal quantities of chicken or turkey and ham cut in julienne strips (the Colonel suggests also using tongue or *foie gras* similarly cut). Sandwich them between day-old slices of bread, thinly cut and spread with *ravigote* butter.

Half the suggested amount of herbs and butter is about right for 12 slices of average-sized sandwich bread. Because the chicken is cut into small strips, it doesn't matter if the less glamorously shaped pickings off the carcass are used.

Right: Chicken Sandwiches with Ravigote Butter.

Coronation Chicken

Devised for the coronation of Queen Elizabeth II in 1953, this could be regarded as a variation on the theme of chicken mayonnaise. The industrial versions used as sandwich fillings in the 1990s did few favours for what is, when well made, a delicious dish, which most people love.

2 tablespoons sunflower oil
1 small onion, peeled and very finely chopped
1 dessertspoon curry powder (mild Madras)
generous 1 tablespoon mango chutney, rubbed through a sieve
250g (9oz) mayonnaise, home-made or good-quality bottled
1 cold roast chicken, skinned, boned and divided into neat,
    roughly bite-sized chunks
flaked almonds, toasted until golden brown
salt and pepper
lettuce leaves, lightly dressed with oil and vinegar, to serve

Serves 4–6

Heat the oil and fry the onion very gently until translucent. Stir in the curry powder and continue to cook gently until it loses its raw smell. Remove from the heat and allow to cool.

Stir in the mango chutney and the mayonnaise to make a thick, lightly curried cold sauce. Taste and adjust the seasoning. Arrange the chicken pieces on top of the lettuce leaves and pour the curried mayonnaise over. Scatter the almonds on top.

Left: Coronation Chicken.

Turkey

In Britain, it's difficult to think of turkey without thinking of Christmas. When these birds first arrived, shortly after European explorers discovered the Americas, they were an exotic curiosity. However, they fitted into a recognisable place in the eating habits of the time – as a large bird among the many already served at the tables of the rich at great feasts and important occasions. Christmas was undoubtedly one of these; the association between the two developed early but not exclusively until the late 19th century.

Prices for turkeys were cited in London markets by the 1550s, when they were also mentioned in conjunction with Christmas by Thomas Tusser. By the 17th century turkeys had spread across England – partly because they were novelties, albeit difficult ones (they detest wet conditions). Rearing turkeys became a speciality of East Anglia, especially Norfolk, in the 17th and 18th centuries. The birds were turned loose on the stubble after harvest to fatten on any stray corn, and were then driven (on foot) to the Christmas markets of large towns and to London.

Like chickens, turkeys were seasonal to some extent. Turkey poults (young birds) were very expensive in early spring, but prices dropped as the summer wore on, and into the autumn. But even in the first half of the 19th century, demand was by far the strongest in mid-December, Eliza Acton remarked 'The great demand for turkeys in England towards Christmas, and the care which they require in being reared, causes them to be brought much less abundantly into the markets when young, than they are in foreign countries; in many of which they are very plentiful and very cheap.'

Roasting a turkey in the past was obviously regarded as almost as much of an undertaking as it is now. Suggested spit-roasting times are relatively short by our standards. However, cooks were always entreated to make sure that the bird was fully done, preferably by allowing it time to come to room temperature before roasting – a reflection of the fact that the birds were mostly cooked in winter, and that old-fashioned larders were chilly. Another point noted by cookery writers in the past was that the sinews in a turkey's legs should be pulled (large birds develop tough sinews to keep them upright), and that doing so could be difficult. Mrs Roundell suggested shutting the bird's legs in the crack of a door, with one person inside holding the bird, and the other outside, pulling on the legs. We may be squeamish about such things, but a cook in a good household would have to know how to carry out such procedures in order to serve a bird that was considered properly dressed.

Turkeys were trussed like chicken for roasting, the wings and legs tied close to the body, sometimes with the gizzard of the bird under one wing, and its liver under the other. This English mode exasperated the Frenchman Alexis Soyer, who in 1849 considered that treating the liver this way would spoil the look of the bird once roasted (because it would drip juices down the side as it cooked), but the 'liver-wing' was considered a delicacy until the mid-19th century.

Stuffings and forcemeats of various descriptions were almost always used with turkeys by the 18th century, mostly in the crop (at the front of the breast). A standard English type of stuffing with herbs and lemon was one option, but mixtures using cooked veal, pork sausagemeat or chestnuts were often given. Pork products of various kinds, including sausages, have been consistently used with turkeys over the centuries. Eliza Acton suggested that the body of the bird could be filled with chestnuts stewed with ham or bacon. For a more elaborate dish, the bird could be made into a galantine by boning it, filling with forcemeat and sewing it up again before cooking. Hannah Glasse, in 1747, gave an early recipe for this under the title 'To roast a turky the genteel way', using a highly seasoned forcemeat based on veal or chicken. More usually wrapped in a cloth and simmered in water, this is a good way of dealing with a small bird.

The idea of a turkey as a special feast remains, despite intensive production and the demise of stubble-fed fowl. Acquire a well-produced bird and cook it gently (the recipe on page 86 is a revelation), and think about the feasts of fowl – wild and domestic – enjoyed in the houses of the Elizabethan nobility.

Buying, Storage and Preparation

Even a small turkey weighs 4–5kg (8½–11lb) and will feed 8 people easily; monster birds of 8–10kg (17½–22lb) are quite usual, and likely to leave even a large family with a substantial quantity of leftovers. Most commercial turkeys are white-feathered, largely because British consumers, over the years, have shown a dislike for the dark pits left on the skin after black feathers have been removed. If this does not bother you, and the idea of a bird with slightly more flavour and slightly less breast meat appeals, try to find a Norfolk Black from one of the few suppliers who still take an interest in this breed. The internet is your best method for tracking these down, unless you happen to know someone who moves in the poultry-fancying or turkey-breeding worlds. A well-flavoured alternative is a Kelly Bronze, bred by the family after which it is named to have a deeper flavour than standard commercial stock, and reared under specified conditions (again, the internet will point you towards a supplier).

Remove a turkey from the packaging in which it arrives. Put it on a large dish or in a tin, dry with kitchen paper if it seems wet, and also blot the inside, checking that there are no odds and ends that shouldn't be there. Pick over it for any stray feathers and stubs, cover loosely and store in the bottom of the refrigerator. Remove it and allow it to reach room temperature for 1–2 hours before roasting.

Prepare stuffing in advance if it needs to cool before using. Stuff the crop only (not the body), to avoid the risk of heat not penetrating fully to the centre and the potential for food poisoning. The skin on the neck of the bird will have been left long to make a flap that can be folded over the back and sewn down to keep the stuffing in; you might like to make sure this is neatly trimmed. For birds generally, the cook was sometimes instructed to remove the merrythought (wishbone) beforehand, on the grounds that it makes carving easier. Turkey is perhaps the one bird where this is worth the effort (unless your family tradition is to pull the bone and make a wish across the Christmas table). Under the skin, you will find a line between the flesh of the breast (translucent and slightly pink) and the fat (opaque and creamy), forming the apex of a triangle with the point where the wishbone joins the keel of the breastbone. Cut along these lines with a small sharp knife to free the two long sides of the bone and then work the knife carefully around the top and the points where it meets the wing bones, one at either side. Whether you remove the wishbone or not, add the chosen stuffing, moulding it to give the bird a nice plump breast, and pull the skin back, sewing it down with thin string to prevent the stuffing escaping. Add the weight of the stuffing to that of the bird when you calculate the cooking time.

Roasting and Carving

Large turkeys are heavy and difficult to handle when hot. Make sure you have a large enough roasting tin and – if buying very large birds – that the turkey is not too big for the oven. It is also important that turkeys are properly cooked.

The meat has a tendency to dryness, which long cooking exacerbates. Methods suggested for counteracting this include marinating, barding, basting, and slow, gentle cooking. Marinating overnight in flavoured brine can help retain moisture. Bard with fat bacon, a butter-soaked cloth, or simply smear softened butter over the breast of the bird (especially if you intend to cook it lying on its back all the time). Basting by pouring the cooking juices and fat back over the bird fairly frequently is a good idea. Also effective is to start cooking with it lying on its side and then turning it, before finally turning it on to its back to complete cooking. Temperatures and times recommended for turkey vary enormously, and depend partly on size. As a guideline, I use 170°C, 325°F, Gas mark 3 for 30 minutes per 500g but, as ever, be guided by personal experience, the quirks of individual ovens and instinct at the time.

When the bird is fully cooked, leave it to rest, covered, in a warm place. To carve, take slices of breast from back to front. Carve any stuffing or forcemeat in the crop across in slices. Then take off the legs and the wings (with a narrow outer portion of breast attached), and divide like those of a chicken, carving slices off the thighs and drumsticks.

Turkey Giblet Stock

Heat a little olive oil in a fairly large saucepan and add around 100g (4oz) bacon. Allow it to fry gently until it loses its translucency. Chop 1 peeled shallot, a leek, a celery stick, a carrot, a turnip, a handful of mushroom stalks and some fresh parsley. Add to the pan and turn up the heat. Cook briskly, stirring frequently, until the pieces begin to brown. Add the giblets of the bird, pour in 400ml (14fl oz) chicken stock or water, then bring to the boil and simmer gently for about 1 hour. Strain, discarding the debris, and skim off any fat. This stock can be prepared in advance and kept chilled.

Alderman in Chains

This is based on a recipe given by Mrs Roundell in 1898, although the idea of a green
herb stuffing goes back much further. These quantities are about right for a small turkey.

1 oven-ready turkey, about
    4.5–5kg (10–11lb)
75g (3oz) unsalted butter, softened
8 sausages in a string
splash of Giblet Stock (see page 84),
    to deglaze
1–2 tablespoons arrowroot

FOR THE GREEN HERB STUFFING
150g (5oz) stale breadcrumbs

1 dessertspoon finely chopped fresh
    thyme or marjoram leaves
1 tablespoon finely chopped parsley
grated zest of ½ lemon (preferably
    unwaxed)
75g (3oz) beef suet, or unsalted
    butter broken into small pieces
1–2 medium eggs, beaten
1 teaspoon salt
freshly ground black pepper

Serves 8

For the green herb stuffing, mix all the ingredients together, adding the eggs last, in stages; the consistency should be soft, but not too wet. Use the mixture to stuff the crop of the turkey, then sew the skin closed over it.

Preheat the oven to 170°C, 325°F, Gas mark 3. Calculate the roasting time (see page 84). Spread the softened butter over the bird and season well. Place it on one side in the roasting tin. Cook for about 45 minutes, basting at intervals of about 15 minutes. Turn it on to the other side and baste well, then cook for another 45 minutes. Finally, turn it on to its back and baste again, then protect the breast with a piece of foil and continue to cook, basting regularly.

About 45 minutes before the end of cooking time, put the sausages into a baking tray (don't cut the links) and put them in the oven to cook.

About 15 minutes before the end of cooking time, remove the foil from the turkey, baste again, and allow the skin to brown. When the bird is fully cooked, remove it to a warmed platter and allow to rest for about 20 minutes. Check the progress of the sausages, but don't move them around too much – the aim is to keep them in a string.

Skim off any fat from the cooking juices and add the stock. Bring to the boil, scraping round the roasting tin to collect any browned bits from the sides. Mix the arrowroot with a little cold water and add to the juices. Heat gently until they boil and the arrowroot has become translucent and thickened the gravy slightly.

Present the bird with the string of cooked sausages draped over the breast of the bird or around its front – the 'chains' of the pouting alderman.

The Italian Way of Roasting a Turkey

4.5kg (10lb) oven-ready turkey
about 30g (1oz) unsalted butter
2–3 rashers unsmoked bacon
1 large carrot, chopped
1 onion, peeled and chopped
1 small white turnip, chopped
2 celery sticks, chopped
3 garlic cloves, peeled and chopped
2 large fresh rosemary sprigs
4–5 cloves
500ml (18fl oz) Giblet Stock
   (see page 84)
1–2 tablespoons arrowroot
salt

FOR THE STUFFING
unsalted butter
about 100g (4oz) unsmoked
   bacon, rind removed, chopped
   in small pieces
about 100g (4oz) good-quality
   sausage meat
100g (4oz) chestnut purée
3 prunes, pitted and chopped
1 small hard pear, peeled
   and chopped
75ml (3fl oz) Marsala
salt and pepper

Serves 8

To make the stuffing, melt the butter, add the bacon and sausage meat and fry gently for a few minutes. Stir in the chestnut purée, prunes, pear and Marsala and season with a little salt and plenty of pepper. Cool and use to stuff the crop of the turkey.

To cook the turkey, use a stout roasting tin. Smear the butter over the base, and put the bacon and vegetables in. Nestle the garlic, rosemary and cloves among the pieces. Put the turkey on its back on top of this, and add enough stock to cover the base of the tin. Season the bird. Cover the whole tin with a sheet of tinfoil, crimping it firmly around the edges. Put the tin on the hob on the lowest heat – use two rings, both turned very low, one at each end of the tin. Braise the bird, very gently, for about 1½ hours. Check occasionally to make sure it is not drying up, adding more liquid if necessary.

Preheat the oven to 180–190°C, 350–375°F, Gas mark 4–5. Move the turkey, still in the covered container, into the oven, and cook for another 45–60 minutes. Remove the foil, baste well, salt the skin and finish roasting, uncovered, for another 45 minutes. Add a little liquid if the juices show signs of drying out. Once the bird is cooked, remove it to a warm serving dish and allow to rest. Tip everything left in the tin through a sieve, catching the juices in a bowl. Press with the back of a wooden spoon to extract any liquid, but don't rub the solids through – they can be discarded. Put the juices in a pan. Add about 250ml (9fl oz) stock (or more, if you want lots of gravy and the depth of flavour will take it). Finish by slaking the arrowroot with a little cold water; stir this into the gravy and reheat until just boiling and lightly thickened.

Chestnut Forcemeat

Chestnut stuffings go back at least as far as the first half of the 19th century in English cookery. This one is based on a recipe given by Eliza Acton (in 1845) and is good for turkey and game.

150g (5oz) chestnut purée
75g (3oz) unsmoked bacon, rind removed,
   cut in to small pieces
50g (2oz) stale white breadcrumbs
grated zest of ½ lemon (preferably unwaxed)
a pinch of freshly grated nutmeg
a pinch of cayenne pepper
1 medium egg
a little stock or milk
1 teaspoon salt

Serves 8

Mix together all the ingredients except the stock to make a smooth paste. If it seems a little on the dry side, stir in some stock to slacken the mixture a little.

    This mixture can be used as stuffing or made into 8 little cakes, floured and then fried gently.

French Forcemeat

An alternative stuffing for turkey, for those who like a meaty, savoury flavour. It can also be used for veal, or for rabbit or hare. For veal, use more sweet herbs; for rabbit or hare, add 300ml (10fl oz) cream.

The original of this delicious recipe was given by John Thacker in 1758. About a century later, Eliza Acton was quoting essentially the same recipe, although without the typically 18th-century addition of anchovies. I've left them in, as it seems to me to suit modern tastes. Thacker was not specific about the uses of his recipe, but suggested replacing the veal with beef suet for stuffing a turkey – which would render the mixture inedibly fatty to us. Better to stick with veal, or if that is unobtainable, use chicken. Cooked lean veal left over from a roast can be used.

75g (3oz) unsalted butter

2–3 open mushrooms, chopped (optional)

the liver of the bird, chopped (optional)

150g (5oz) lean cooked veal or chicken, minced

1 large teaspoon chopped fresh parsley

½ teaspoon fresh thyme leaves

grated zest of ½ lemon (preferably unwaxed)

2 anchovies, chopped

a generous pinch of freshly grated nutmeg

a pinch of cayenne pepper

a pinch of ground mace

50g (2oz) stale white breadcrumbs

a little stock or gravy

30g (1oz) unsmoked bacon, chopped

1 medium egg yolk

salt

To stuff a small 4–5kg (9–10lb) turkey

Heat 50g (2oz) of the butter in a small frying pan. Cook the mushrooms and liver for a few minutes, then add the veal or chicken, parsley, thyme, lemon zest and anchovies. Season fairly generously with nutmeg and add a pinch of cayenne, a little mace and the breadcrumbs. Allow to cool, then tip into a food processor and whizz to a paste, adding a little stock if the mixture seems dry. Mix in the remaining butter, bacon and the egg yolk.

Note that Thacker says, 'take care you don't season it too high'. The best way to find out is to fry a trial spoonful and taste it. Only then add extra salt if you consider it necessary, as the anchovies and bacon will have contributed some already.

Almond Sauce

Another excellent recipe from The Gentle Art of Cookery *by Mrs Leyel and Miss Hartley (1925), whose book also provided The Italian Way of Roasting a Turkey (see page 86). Nut sauces for all sorts of meat recur in Middle Eastern and Indian cookery. This has no obvious affiliations, nor do the authors say where it comes from (although it is similar to Colonel Kenney-Herbert's Cashew Nut Sauce, page 75). It is delicious and haters of bread sauce will probably enjoy it very much.*

30g (1oz) unsalted butter
100g (4oz) ground almonds
30g (1oz) plain flour
250–300ml (9–10fl oz) stock
a pinch of ground mace
2 tablespoons single cream (optional)
a little salt

Serves 6

Melt the butter in a heavy saucepan and stir the almonds in over low heat. Cook very gently, stirring all the time, until the almonds are browned and toasted. Stir in the flour, then add the stock and continue to cook and stir until the mixture comes to the boil. Season with a little mace (which really does enhance this recipe) and salt. Finish by adding cream if you have some available.

Leftovers

Christmas dinner is possibly the one time of the year when the average British household finds itself with vast amounts of leftovers sitting in the refrigerator and demanding ingenuity in the using up, before everyone gets completely bored with the taste of turkey in curries, fricassees, pies, sandwiches and soup … For sandwiches, see also Chicken Sandwiches with Ravigote Butter, page 80.

Devilled Turkey

Particularly good with the brown meat of turkey, devilling was a popular way of dealing with all sorts of meat, including leftovers, from the late 18th to the mid-20th century. A spicy paste was used to marinate the food, which was then grilled. The idea seems to have been forgotten, maybe because devils were often made too hot. Although some recipes for devil pastes now seem tame, E.S. Dallas complains in Kettner's Book of the Table *(1877) of the 'great fault that devilry knows no bounds … if the devil is not moderate he destroys the palate …' and he advised caution with the pepper. This recipe is based on one in* Mrs A. B. Marshall's Cookery Book*, a classic of the late 19th century.*

about 250g (9oz) cooked turkey
2 teaspoons Dijon mustard
½ teaspoon English mustard
    (made up, not powder)
½ teaspoon salt

2 heaped dessertspoons mango
    chutney – any large pieces of
    fruit in the chutney chopped fine
cayenne pepper, to taste
freshly ground black pepper

Serves 2

Prepare the turkey, pulling it into long narrow pieces. The skin can be left on, as it crisps nicely under the grill. Mix the mustards, salt and chutney, adding as much cayenne as you feel desirable (try ¼ teaspoon if unsure) and a generous grind of black pepper. Rub the paste into the turkey pieces and leave in a cool place for 1–2 hours.

To cook, put the pieces under a preheated moderate grill for a few minutes. Keep a close eye on them and turn a couple of times, until they are well heated through. Any skin should turn quite crisp, and the edges of the pieces may brown, but try not to let them char. Alternatively, put them in a single layer in an ovenproof dish and bake in a hot oven, 220°C, 425°F, Gas mark 7, for 7–10 minutes.

Serve hot with rice and more chutney, or scatter over a salad of mixed leaves.

White Devil

In The Tenth Muse *(1992), a collection of recipes from people he encountered while a member of the diplomatic corps, Sir Henry Luke gives a recipe specifically intended for white meat from turkey or other fowls. The result is pleasingly creamy and mildly piquant, and the heat can be increased by adding more slivers of fresh green or red chilli.*

280ml (9½fl oz) single cream
2 tablespoons Worcestershire sauce
1 teaspoon English mustard or to taste
250g (9oz) cooked turkey breast meat,
    cut in neat pieces
fresh green or red chillies (optional)
salt

Serves 4

Put the cream in a saucepan and mix in the Worcestershire sauce and mustard. Heat rapidly until it boils. Stir in the turkey meat and allow to cook, very gently, until it is thoroughly hot. If using fresh chilli, remove the strings and seeds and cut the flesh into fine slivers. Add to the pan, then taste and correct the seasoning.

Serve with boiled rice and a salad.

Salsa for Turkey

Sometimes a 'sauce piquant' was served with devilled food in the 19th century. Recipes for it are based on a reduction of shallots and vinegar in butter, made into a flour-thickened sauce, which was further livened up with pepper, chilli or chopped gherkins. To us, the flavour is a bit contrived, but the vinegar-onion reduction suggested a tomato salsa – which usually contains raw onions, not to everyone's taste.

1 small shallot, peeled and very finely chopped
4 tablespoons white wine vinegar
1–2 tablespoons olive oil
1 beef tomato, skin and seeds removed, finely diced
1 garlic clove, peeled and crushed
a little chopped fresh red chilli
a pinch of granulated sugar
salt

Serves 2–4

Put the shallot and vinegar in a small pan and boil rapidly until the vinegar has evaporated. Pour into a small bowl and stir in the oil and tomato. Add the garlic and the chilli to taste, plus a pinch of sugar and a little salt.

This can be served with Devilled Turkey (see page 90), or added to a Club Sandwich (see below).

Club Sandwich

Use three slices of toast per sandwich; spread the bottom layer with a little mayonnaise, add salad leaves (flat lettuce or lamb's lettuce), and 2–3 rashers crisp bacon; add a second layer of toast, then spread with a little more mayonnaise, top with thinly sliced turkey breast and a layer of salsa and top with a final layer of toast. Press down firmly and cut obliquely to make triangular sandwiches.

Curry

There are so many curry pastes and marinades available that it may seem a bit redundant to give a recipe, but here is a delicious one based on Colonel Kenney-Herbert's spicing for a mild, coconut-flavoured Ceylon curry (he was emphatic that only fish, shellfish, veal or chicken should be added, but most things that work for chicken, work for turkey as well). It can be spiced up with more chilli if desired.

250–300g (9–10oz) onions, peeled and very finely chopped

50g (2oz) unsalted butter

1 teaspoon ground turmeric

2 teaspoons ground coriander

1 teaspoon ground cinnamon

½ teaspoon ground cardamom seeds

½ teaspoon chilli powder

½ teaspoon freshly ground black pepper

½ teaspoon salt

1 tablespoon grated fresh root ginger

400ml (14fl oz) coconut milk

400g (14oz) cooked turkey, cut in bite-sized chunks

Serves 4

Put the onions and butter in a heatproof casserole and fry gently until the onions begin to turn gold. Add the spices and salt and cook gently for about 5 minutes, then add the ginger. Stir in the coconut milk and bring to the boil to make a smooth sauce. Allow this to cook gently for a few minutes longer, then stir in the turkey and continue to simmer for about 15 minutes so that the sauce reduces a little. It shouldn't be too runny.

Serve with rice and salad.

Turkey Pie

Turkey, chicken or veal and ham combinations are all traditional in pies in English cookery. Add mushrooms, or make a particularly good (if expensive) version by adding some of the white truffle and porcini paste sold in jars in Italian delicatessens.

40g (1½oz) unsalted butter

150g (5oz) button mushrooms, sliced

40g (1½oz) plain flour

350ml (12fl oz) well-flavoured turkey stock

shortcrust pastry made with 100g (4oz) unsalted butter
    and lard mixed, and 200g (7oz) plain flour

40g (1½oz) white truffle and porcini paste (optional)

200–250g (7–9oz) cooked turkey, cut in neat pieces

125g (4½oz) cooked ham or gammon, cut in dice

1 medium egg, beaten

salt and pepper

Serves 4–6

Melt the butter in a saucepan and cook the mushrooms until all the liquid they exude has evaporated, but don't allow them to brown. Stir in the flour to make a roux, then add the stock gradually, stirring to produce a sauce. Season to taste and allow to cool.

When ready to bake, preheat the oven to 200°C, 400°F, Gas mark 6 and put a metal baking sheet in to heat.

Roll two-thirds of the pastry fairly thin and use it to line a pie dish about 20cm (8in) in diameter.

If using the truffle paste, mix it with the turkey meat. Distribute this, and the ham, over the pastry. Spoon the sauce in on top. Roll out the remaining pastry and use to cover the pie, sealing and crimping the edges. Cut a hole in the top for the steam to escape and decorate the surface of the pie with leaves made from the pastry trimmings. Brush with beaten egg.

Put the pie on the preheated baking sheet and cook for 15–20 minutes to set and crisp the pastry. Then reduce the heat to 180°C, 350°F, Gas mark 4, and bake for a further 20–25 minutes.

Serve hot or cold.

Turkey Soup

Turkey bones make excellent stock. The slower it is cooked, the better – put the stockpot in a very low oven after the contents have come to the boil, or use a slow cooker, in which case you should get a lovely clear golden broth. It can be used to make this 21st-century version of Eliza Acton's 'Economical turkey soup'. Hers was beefed up (literally) with some fresh beef when making the stock, and served with a little boiled rice in the broth. We'd consider the beef an extravagance, but the suggestion she made about adding ham and 'catsup' (a catch-all name for various condiment sauces imported directly from the Far East, or based on attempts to imitate these) suggested south-east Asian flavours.

1 litre (1¾ pints) well-flavoured turkey stock
a few celery leaves, finely chopped
about 100g (4oz) ham, diced
1 fresh red chilli pepper, finely diced
2 teaspoons nam pla (Thai fish sauce)
100g (4oz) cooked rice
salt
chopped fresh coriander
lime zest, preferably unwaxed, cut in fine slivers (optional)

Serves 4

Put the turkey stock in a large pan and bring to the boil. Add the celery leaves, ham, chilli pepper and nam pla, and cook for a few minutes. Add the cooked rice just before serving and let it heat through (it can be added earlier, but it makes the stock lose some of its clarity). Taste and add more salt if necessary. Ladle into bowls and add a sprinkle of chopped coriander and a little lime zest to each serving.

Goose

Christmas is coming, the geese are getting fat ... Domestic geese are probably descended from wild geese native to Europe. Even the poorest of the rural poor could keep a few, pastured on common land, and for many centuries they were Christmas food. It was a goose that Ebenezer Scrooge bought for the Cratchit family in Charles Dickens' *A Christmas Carol* (1843), but a century later turkeys had supplanted them on the festive table.

Geese are resistant to attempts to farm them intensively. They need space and grass to graze on, and they remain highly seasonal as food. Until the 19th century, geese were eaten during the autumn as well. Like most birds, the young hatched in spring were at their peak in autumn, still tender, and fat because they had had all summer to feed. A stubble-fattened goose was a traditional item for a Michaelmas dinner – 29th September – was an important date because it was one of the 'quarter' days of the English calendar, when rents and debts were paid. This was the start of the season when geese were at their best, which ran through until Christmas. Young birds were also eaten as 'green geese' around Whitsuntide, a habit we have lost entirely.

In the middle of the 20th century, goose became difficult to buy as the poultry industry intensified. Turkey became the norm and the small mixed farms that used to rear a few geese every year became uneconomic. Interest in geese has revived recently, partly because they have a deep, rich flavour, quite different from turkey, and partly because of their resistance to intensive systems.

In the past, geese were cooked by a variety of methods, but roasting was always a favourite because it both removes the copious fat and produces a delicious crisp skin. Carving a goose was something of a ceremony in the 19th century. The carver started by cutting away the 'apron', the skin below the breast, and pouring a glass of claret mixed with mustard into the bird, before removing some of the stuffing. A 'graceful and well-skilled' carver reckoned never to have to turn a bird on its side to disjoint the leg, but it was acknowledged that this was sometimes a necessity when carving goose, as the hip sockets are difficult to reach with the carving knife.

Sage and onion stuffing seems to have been the invariable accompaniment – to the extent that some cuts of other meats cooked with it were sometimes called 'mock goose'. Cooks always differed about how apparent the flavourings should be. In the mid-18th century, Hannah Glasse warned 'never put Onion into any thing unless you are sure every body loves it.' Colonel Kenney-Herbert and Mrs Roundell, in the late 19th century, both appear to have considered sage objectionably strong, and subdued its flavour by blanching. Potato stuffings for goose, with apple, onion, shallot or herbs, are mentioned in several mid-19th century cookery books, and some variation on this is an excellent idea. Green geese were never stuffed, but until the mid-19th century were often served with sorrel sauce – worth trying, should you have a green goose to hand.

Buying, Storage and Preparation

One company, Gressingham, dominates large-scale goose production, but there are a number of small producers scattered across Britain, especially in East Anglia and the South-West. A goose from a local butcher may well have been produced quite locally and on a relatively small scale. Most people who like goose enough to eat it annually try to find a farmer who raises them as a hobby or on a small commercial scale, and then stick with that supplier over the years. Frozen goose is available, and it is possible to produce a reasonable result with one, but somehow they never seem to crisp up as much as the fresh item, so avoid if possible (should you want a goose for Michaelmas, though, it may be the only option). Large supermarkets stock a limited number of geese around Christmas.

A small goose weighs about 5kg (11lb) a large one about 7kg (15lb). The meat over the breast is a relatively shallow layer, so despite their size they really don't serve more than 6 people (a big one might stretch to 8 people), with little in the way of leftover meat. On the other hand, the meat is both deeper in flavour and much richer than turkey, so portions can be smaller, and you will have enough goose fat to roast potatoes every Sunday for the rest of the year, and bones for good stock.

In common with all meat, it is best to remove any wrappings as soon as possible. Geese are now usually deprived of their copious down and the last of their feathers by waxing, and are generally very clean. However, it is always a good idea to pick over them for strays and the odd bit of wax.

Wash the giblets. Examine the liver to check that the gall bladder has been removed – if it is still there, discard it, along with any bits of liver it has stained green. If you don't want to add the liver to the stuffing, make it into pâté by frying it in a generous quantity of butter, adding a peeled and crushed garlic clove, a little brandy and seasoning and then whizzing it in a food processor.

Goose Giblet Stock

1 tablespoon fat from the goose, or some unsalted butter,
    lard or unsmoked bacon fat
the giblets of the bird
2–3 rashers unsmoked bacon, chopped
1 small carrot, chopped
½ onion, peeled and chopped
½ celery stick, peeled and chopped
100ml (3½fl oz) red wine or 2–3 tablespoons Madeira
1 bouquet garni of fresh thyme, parsley and marjoram
400ml (14fl oz) chicken stock or water

Heat the fat in a saucepan and add the giblets and bacon. Fry until translucent, then add the chopped vegetables. Cook briskly, stirring frequently, until beginning to brown. Pour in the wine or Madeira and cook until reduced by half. Add the bouquet garni and the chicken stock. Bring to a simmer and cook gently for 1 hour. Strain and skim off any fat.

Roast Goose

Goose has a skin that crisps up wonderfully on cooking. For optimum results, use a boiling water treatment similar to that for pork crackling (see page 51). About 6–12 hours before cooking, remove the goose from any packaging and stand it on a rack over the sink. Prick the skin, especially the parts that have fat deposits underneath, using a skewer or a knife with a narrow blade. Heat a large kettleful of water and as soon as it boils, pour the water over the bird (turn the goose so that both back and front get the treatment). Pat the bird dry very thoroughly with kitchen paper. Also dry the inside, taking especial care in the neck area, which tends to contain blood clots – wipe to get rid of these. Then put the goose in a cool airy place, or in the refrigerator; cover lightly with greaseproof paper or a clean tea towel.

Geese are large birds and the amount of fat they yield during cooking is startling if you are unaccustomed to it. Make sure the oven is big enough. You will need a deep roasting tin, a rack, a pair of sturdy oven gloves or gauntlets, and a capacious bowl for the fat. A supply of heavy-duty tinfoil is also useful, especially if the roasting tin is on the skimpy side. Allow 30 minutes per 500g.

1 goose
stuffing, as required
Giblet Stock (see page 97)
2 tablespoons arrowroot
salt and pepper

Serves 6

About 1 hour before you want to start cooking the bird, allow it to come to room temperature. Preheat the oven to 220°C, 425°F, Gas mark 7. Rub the bird with salt and pepper and stuff the body if required. Place the goose on a rack in a deep roasting tin. Start it breast downwards. Use tinfoil to extend the tin under any of the goose that projects over the edge (it's also useful for wrapping round wing tips and ends of drumsticks if they show signs of browning too fast).

Put the goose into the oven and cook for 30 minutes, then turn the heat down to 180–190°C, 350–375°F, Gas mark 4–5 and continue to roast. After 30 minutes, remove from the oven and pour or ladle the fat out of the roasting tin into a bowl. Turn the goose on to its back. Return it to the oven and continue to cook. Keep checking the amount of fat in the roasting tin, and pour it off into a bowl from time to time. Once the bird is fully cooked, remove it from the oven and allow to rest for about 20 minutes.

To finish the gravy, pour off the fat, returning any browned cooking juices and sediment to the tin. Pour in the giblet stock, stir to deglaze and bring to the boil. Slake the arrowroot with a little water and pour into the gravy. Bring it back to boiling point to thicken. Taste and correct the seasoning, then strain into a gravy boat.

Chestnut and Prune Stuffing

Chestnut stuffing is more commonly associated with turkey, but can also be very good with goose. The same is true for prunes, which are quite often used with goose in continental Europe. Like potato stuffing, this didn't make much of an impact in British cookery until the mid-20th century.

15g (½oz) unsalted butter
1–2 shallots, peeled and finely chopped
1 garlic clove, peeled and crushed
200–250g (7–9oz) chestnut purée (tinned is fine)
200–250g (7–9oz) sausage meat
about 12 prunes (ready-to-eat, or soaked dried ones), pitted
2 large apples (Cox's or a dryish, aromatic eating apple), peeled,
   cored and cut in thick slices
1 scant teaspoon salt
freshly ground black pepper

Enough to stuff a 5–7kg (11–15lb) goose

Melt the butter in a small pan and fry the shallots and garlic lightly. Put the chestnut purée in a bowl and break it up. Mix in the shallots and garlic, sausage meat, salt and a generous seasoning of pepper.

Put half this mixture into the goose, then add the prunes and apples in a layer, and spread the remainder of the stuffing over them.

Potato and Apple Stuffing

Mashed potatoes are excellent for stuffing goose. Alexis Soyer advocated them in the mid-19th century, in combination with apples, although the idea of using them didn't really become popular in English cookery until the middle of the 20th century.

75g (3oz) unsalted butter
1 large onion, peeled and chopped
about 600g (1¼lb) floury potatoes, peeled and cut into chunks
2 garlic cloves, peeled and crushed
1 tablespoon chopped fresh sage
2 large apples (Cox's or a dryish, aromatic eating apple)
    peeled, cored and cut into chunks
generous 1 teaspoon salt
freshly ground black pepper

Enough to stuff a 5–7kg (11–15lb) goose

Melt the butter in a large frying pan, then add the onion and cook gently until it begins to brown.

Boil the potatoes and mash. Stir in the cooked onions, the crushed garlic, sage, salt and a generous seasoning of pepper. Mix the pieces of apple through the mixture, and use to stuff the goose.

Leftovers

Alexis Soyer's Hashed Goose

There are few recipes for using up the meat from a cold roast goose in the British repertoire – perhaps because the bird doesn't feed that many people at one sitting. Even the great Alexis Soyer flagged somewhat when contemplating leftover goose, suggesting this simple recipe.

15g (½oz) unsalted butter or goose fat
½ small onion, peeled and finely chopped
1 dessertspoon plain flour
250ml (9fl oz) well-flavoured stock, preferably goose (see page 97)

about 250g (9oz) leftover cooked goose, cut in slices
2–3 fresh sage leaves, torn into pieces
salt and pepper

Serves 2

Melt the butter in a large saucepan and fry the onion gently until soft. Stir in the flour and cook for a few minutes, then add the stock and stir to make a sauce. Add the cooked goose and the sage. Simmer gently until all is hot, then taste and adjust the seasoning. Serve with mashed potato.

Pickled Pears

400g (14oz) hard pears (underripe Conference, or similar)
100g (4oz) light soft brown sugar
grated zest of ½ lemon (preferably unwaxed)

100ml (3½fl oz) white wine vinegar or cider vinegar
4 cloves, bruised
10 black peppercorns, bruised

Makes 400g (14oz)

Peel, core and cut the pears into chunks. Place all the ingredients in a pan and bring to the boil. Boil, uncovered, for 20–30 minutes, or until the pieces of pear are soft. Mash them into the liquid a little to help them break down. The result should have a slightly jammy consistency.

Eat immediately, or keep in the refrigerator for up to 2 weeks. Serve with cold roast goose.

Goose Salad

Don't put any large pieces of goose skin in the stockpot. Remove it from the bird and cut into neat pieces about 1cm (½in) wide and 2cm (¾in) long. Put these in a baking tray with a lip (they will yield quite a lot of fat), sprinkle with salt, and cook in a hot oven at 220°C, 425°F, Gas mark 7. Look at them after 7–10 minutes, when they should have crisped up. Thicker pieces may need a little longer. Drain on kitchen paper and scatter over mashed potatoes, or use in a salad, such as this one, with any bits of leftover cooked goose.

1 large eating apple, such as Cox's or a russet
1½ celery sticks
1 teaspoon very finely chopped onion or shallot
12 walnut halves, broken up a little
cold roast goose, shredded
skin from a roast goose, cooked until crisp

FOR THE DRESSING
1 teaspoon smooth Dijon mustard
a pinch of salt
a little lemon zest (preferably unwaxed), finely grated
1 dessertspoon white wine vinegar or cider vinegar
4 dessertspoons walnut or olive oil

Serves 2

Peel and core the apple, and cut into chunks of about 1cm (½in). Cut the celery into similarly sized pieces. Mix with the onion and the walnut pieces. Add any leftover goose.

Blend the mustard, salt, lemon zest, vinegar and oil to make a dressing and toss with the apple mixture. Scatter the crisp goose skin on top.

Onion Soup

The broth from goose can be used for a vegetable or lentil soup, but is also good for recipes normally requiring a beef stock base. It is better to reduce the stock before using, to concentrate the flavour; I would reduce quantities by slow simmering to about two-thirds of the original.

This is based on an 18th-century recipe from The Experienced English Housewife *by Mrs Raffald (1769), once a housekeeper at Arley Hall in Cheshire and later a professional confectioner and outside caterer in Manchester. A cousin, perhaps, of French onion soup, it responds well to the toast-and-cheese treatment when serving.*

The recipe also works well with beef or duck stock.

2 large Spanish onions – total
   weight about 1kg (2¼lb)
50g (2oz) unsalted butter
1 litre (1¾ pints) well-flavoured
   goose stock
2 medium egg yolks
2 tablespoons cider vinegar
salt and pepper

FOR SERVING
bread for toast (slices from an
   ordinary loaf is fine, but use
   ciabatta or French bread if
   you prefer)
grated Cheddar cheese

Serves 4

Peel the onions, making sure you remove all the papery outer skin plus the layer immediately underneath (which has a tendency to dry out and become hard during cooking). Slice them thinly. Melt the butter in a large pan and add the onions, then stir well and cover. Cook on the lowest possible heat for 45–60 minutes, stirring from time to time. The onions should not colour, but become very soft.

Add the stock, bring to the boil, and simmer gently for about 15 minutes. Taste and add salt and pepper as required. Draw the pan off the heat.

Beat the egg yolks with the vinegar and add to the soup, stirring thoroughly. Once the yolks have been added, the soup should not be allowed to boil again, but should be reheated cautiously until very hot and slightly thickened (don't overdo it, or the egg will curdle).

Just before serving, toast the bread, cover it with grated Cheddar and toast gently until the cheese has melted. Cut into neat pieces and float some on top of each bowl of soup.

Duck

European domestic ducks are probably descended from mallards, the typical wild ducks of the British countryside, the drakes with dark iridescent heads, the ducks speckled mid-brown. Like geese, domestic ducks were often reared by smallholders, the birds congregating around farm or village pond.

For more than 100 years, from the first part of 19th century until the 1920s, Aylesbury in Buckinghamshire was the name associated with ducks for the table in Britain. This breed, large and white-feathered, was raised, according to Isabella Beeton,

'in the abodes of the cottagers. Round the walls of the living-rooms, and of the bedroom even, are fixed rows of wooden boxes, lined with hay; and it is the business of the wife and children to nurse and comfort the feathered lodgers, to feed the little ducklings, and to take the old ones out for an airing.'

The system was similar to one of share-cropping, with the stock being provided by a wealthier partner in the business. As ever, their reputation in London played a part in their fame, Smithfield Market being easily accessible from Buckinghamshire from the mid-19th century onwards. Away from this area, ducks were among the general population of farmyard fowls kept by smallholders when conditions and inclinations allowed.

By World War I, hybrid ducks with Chinese blood were common, and providing competition for the Aylesbury. Subsequently duck farming was subject to the same pressures towards intensification as chicken and turkey production, with high stocking densities, and no access to water for swimming, which is an essential part of duck behaviour. At the same time, hygiene regulations have also reduced economic viability for small producers.

Farmed duck was less seasonal than other birds, obtainable all year round and considered best in early summer. Ducklings (half-grown birds) filled a gap in the calendar in spring, when poultry generally was scarce and the game season had come to an end.

Like other meats, the recipes for use with duck reflect fashion to some extent. The combination of duck with orange appears quite early on, with orange juice being mentioned as a sauce or flavouring for teal (small wild duck) in the mid-17th century by La Varenne. The fruit has been used consistently with duck, both wild and tame, up to the present day. Fashions in more savoury flavours have varied, with typically meaty, savoury combinations in the 18th century; olives were sometimes suggested for flavouring sauces in the 19th century. Ducklings, and sometimes ducks, were served with green peas, either plainly roast and with the peas as an accompaniment, or the two were cooked together in more elaborate dishes. Oranges, olives and peas still make an occasional appearance, but modern palates are exposed to a much wider range of flavours, including those of Asian cultures, in which sweetish, spicy flavours, such as star anise, are combined with duck.

Buying, Storage and Preparation

Intensive methods used for rearing ducks mean that it is difficult to buy a welfare-friendly bird, and less attention seems to have been paid to labelling and transparency about production systems than is true for chicken and turkey. Assume, unless you have proof positive to the contrary, that any duck on sale is intensively produced. Use the internet and local butchers, farmers' markets and farm shops to research suppliers of extensively reared duck.

In the kitchen and on the plate, duck shares many similarities with goose, although it is much smaller. It has only a shallow layer of meat over the breastbone and yields a lot of fat, but has a delicious flavour and a skin that can be roasted to a pleasing crisp texture. Even a relatively large duck will serve only 4 people.

When cooking duck, what everyone wants is crisp skin with moist meat underneath. This is quite difficult to achieve; more usually, the skin is soggy and the meat perfect, or the skin is cooked to a crisp and the meat is completely dried out. One can remove the skin and crisp it up separately (see page 102), but if you want to present a bird at table, intact and croquant, here are a few pointers (my thanks to Caroline Liddell).

Start the process the day before you want to cook. Use a fresh bird (freezing seems to inhibit crisping). Try to part the skin from the fat layer beneath by pulling and pinching all over until it is loosened. Then put the duck on its front on a rack in the sink, boil a kettleful of water and pour the boiling water over the duck. Turn it on to its back, and repeat. Dry the skin, and the inside of the bird, very thoroughly with kitchen paper. Then either hang it somewhere cool and airy, if you have a suitable place, or put it, again on a rack, in the bottom of the refrigerator. The aim is to dry the skin until it has the feel of parchment (some people advise using a hairdryer on a cool setting, or putting the bird in front of a fan). Opinions vary as to whether the skin over fat parts of the bird should be pricked.

Roasting Times

Duck needs a particularly strong heat to start it, so give it 20 minutes at 230°C, 450°F, Gas mark 8 before reducing the heat to 180°C, 350°F, Gas mark 4 and cooking for another 1–1½ hours depending on size; some authorities recommend cooking for much longer, which helps to produce crisp skin but may dry out the meat. Strong poultry shears can be used to cut the bird into quarters when cooked.

Stuffing is a matter of taste; sage and onion was favoured in the past, but use this only if you intend to make a plain gravy (the recipe given on page 148 can be used). I prefer duck without stuffing but with a sauce or marmalade, as described in the individual recipes.

Orange Sauce for Roast Duck

Over the centuries, many cultures have devised ways for cooking and serving duck with fruity and sweet–acid flavours. Seville (bitter, or marmalade) oranges are best, with both tame and wild duck. Their season is very limited – they come on to the market in mid-December and vanish by the end of January – but they can be frozen. This orange sauce is based on one given by Martha Bradley in 1756.

100ml (3½fl oz) port
the cooking juices from the bird, skimmed of fat
juice of 2 Seville oranges
juice of 1 lemon
salt and pepper

Serves 4

Deglaze the roasting tin with the port and pour all into a small pan. Add the juices from cooking the bird and the orange and lemon juice and bring to the boil. Taste, and season with salt and pepper. Serve with the duck and a sweetish vegetable accompaniment, such as roast parsnips, or perhaps boiled potatoes and boiled parsnips mashed together.

Slow Roast Duck Legs with Marmalade

The orange flavourings can also be used to marinate portions of duck.

4 duck legs
1 generous tablespoon bitter orange marmalade
juice of 1 (sweet) orange
juice of 1 lemon
a little stock (optional)
salt and pepper

Serves 4

Put the duck legs in an ovenproof dish that holds them neatly. Mix the marmalade, orange and lemon juices and pour over the duck. Cover and leave in the refrigerator to marinate for 24 hours. Stir from time to time to make sure they are well coated with marinade.

Cook them at 140°C, 275°F, Gas mark 1 for 1¾ hours, turning them after 1 hour. About 15 minutes before the end of cooking time, pour the fat and cooking juices into a bowl and turn up the heat to 170°C, 325°F, Gas mark 3 to crisp the skin.

When the duck legs are ready, remove them to a serving plate. Skim the fat off the reserved cooking juices and use the latter to deglaze the roasting dish (you may want to add a little stock or water to help the process along, but don't overdo it – there should be a relatively small quantity of thin, concentrated gravy). Taste, adjust the seasoning and serve.

John Thacker's Sauce for Roast Duck

John Thacker was cook to the Dean and Chapter of Durham Cathedral, who must have eaten rather well to judge from his recipes. A typically savoury, meaty, early 18th-century sauce for those who don't like sweet–sour combinations. Use with a whole roast duck.

15g (½oz) unsalted butter
1 medium onion, peeled, halved and thinly sliced
scant 1 dessertspoon plain flour
100ml (3½fl oz) red wine
150ml (5fl oz) well-flavoured duck or chicken stock
1 tablespoon salted capers, rinsed
cooking juices from the duck

Serves 4

Melt the butter in a small frying pan. Add the onion and cook fairly quickly, stirring frequently, until it begins to catch and brown slightly. Sprinkle in the flour and stir well. Stir in the red wine, followed by the stock, and keep stirring until the mixture returns to the boil. Add the capers, then turn the heat down and allow to cook gently for at least 20 minutes. Add a little more stock or water if the mixture evaporates too much; it should be fairly thin.

Any juices from roasting the duck, skimmed of fat, can be added just before serving.

Leftovers

Duck, like goose, can yield an astonishing quantity of fat. Pour this off and store in a jar in the refrigerator. Use it for roasting or sautéing potatoes.

One duck serves 4 people very neatly, which may account for the fact that there are very few recipes for using leftover duck in the British cookery repertoire.

Duck and Green Pea Salad

Should the duck skin have refused to crisp up properly, or if there is a fairly large amount of leftover skin, try roasting it in the oven as with the goose skin for the Goose Salad (see page 102). Drain on kitchen paper and scatter over a watercress salad, or mashed potatoes, or try this modern take on the idea of duck with green peas. It can be used to make a small salad for just one person, using the pickings off a duck carcass, or scaled up if more meat is available.

crisp duck skin
50g (2oz) cold duck, picked free of
    skin and fat, cut in slivers
a piece of cucumber about 4cm (1½in)
    long, cut in batons
50g (2oz) cooked peas
1 spring onion, washed, trimmed,
    and cut obliquely in thin slices
1cm (½in) cube fresh root ginger,
    peeled and cut in thin slivers

a piece of red chilli pepper (to taste),
    cut in tiny dice or slivers
chopped green coriander, to garnish

FOR THE DRESSING
½ teaspoon nam pla (Thai fish sauce)
1 teaspoon rice vinegar
2 teaspoons neutral-flavoured oil,
    such as sunflower
a pinch of granulated sugar

Serves 1

Mix the dressing ingredients together, then toss with the duck, skin, cucumber, peas, spring onion, ginger and chilli, and scatter with coriander.

Stewed Duck with Green Peas

This dish usually required a whole fresh duck, but leftover cooked duck could be hashed, like any other meat, and perhaps this is what Isabella Beeton had in mind with her Victorian recipe for stewed duck with green peas. A few ambiguities in the original suggest that she was somewhat distracted when she wrote it out

olive oil, duck fat or unsalted butter
50g (2oz) pancetta or unsmoked bacon, cut in dice or strips
1 shallot, or a bunch of spring onions
1 garlic clove, peeled
200–300g (7–10oz) cold duck, cut in neat pieces
150–200g (5–7oz) peas (frozen ones are fine)
250ml (9fl oz) leftover gravy, or sauce made from 1 dessertspoon
    plain flour, 1 dessertspoon unsalted butter and 250ml (9fl oz)
    duck stock
a pinch of cayenne pepper
a pinch of ground cloves
salt and pepper
chopped parsley, to serve

Serves 2–3

Heat the oil. Add the pancetta or bacon and cook gently until the fat becomes translucent. Peel the shallot or wash and trim the spring onions. Chop finely and add to the pan. Crush the garlic and add this too. Cook gently for a few minutes, then add the duck and the peas (no need to thaw if frozen). Add the gravy and bring to a gentle simmer. Season with the cayenne pepper, cloves and some pepper. Taste before adding salt: the bacon and gravy may be salty enough. Cook gently until the duck is thoroughly hot and the peas are cooked through. Scatter over some parsley and serve with rice.

Beetroot Soup

Beetroot soup is not a British tradition; it arrived, usually as a variation on eastern European borscht, in the early 20th century, as part of an 'international' cookery repertoire. This version is based, very loosely, on one given by Sir Harry Luke in The Tenth Muse *(1992). The soup is better if the stock is clarified, but it is not absolutely essential. The stock does need to be well flavoured, though, so if you can acquire some extra giblets or bones when making it, it will give a better soup. Use duck, goose or beef stock.*

1 large raw beetroot, washed, trimmed and peeled
1 medium carrot, washed, trimmed and peeled
½ small red onion, peeled
2 garlic cloves, peeled
a thumb-sized piece of fresh root ginger, peeled
1 litre (1¾ pints) well-flavoured stock, preferably clarified
2 tablespoons soy sauce
1 tablespoon red wine vinegar
½ teaspoon muscovado sugar
zest of ½ orange (preferably unwaxed), cut in to very thin strips
salt
sour cream, to serve

Serves 3–4

Cut the beetroot and carrot into julienne (long matchstick) strips. Slice the onion very thinly, cut the garlic into fine slivers, and cut the ginger into very thin strips.

Put the stock in a pan and heat, adding all the prepared vegetables. Bring to a simmer and allow to cook for a few minutes. Add the soy sauce, wine vinegar, sugar and orange zest. Taste and check for seasoning: add more of the flavourings if desired, or a little salt if you think the soy sauce hasn't given enough.

Serve with a spoonful of sour cream in each bowl.

Game Birds

Game is our collective term for wild animals and birds that are hunted. It encompasses a wide range – from very small birds suitable for one portion, such as snipe, up to large beasts such as red deer. Game birds in Britain are pheasant, partridge, grouse, pigeon, woodcock, snipe and several species of wild duck. Game animals include rabbit and hare (see page 124), and the meat of several deer species – most importantly red, fallow and roe deer. Wild boar have also been reintroduced to Britain as farmed animals.

Since the Middle Ages, there has always been some management of game species. Methods over the years have included controlling predators and encouraging specific environments, such as grouse moors and parks for deer. Some animals that were originally farmed, such as rabbits, have now made their home in the wild; ones which were once exclusively wild beasts, such as red deer, are now farmed; others, such as pheasants, are reared and fed in such large numbers for shoots that they are semi-domesticated. Game is a category of food with blurred boundaries.

What probably would have surprised our ancestors is the relative cheapness and wide availability of certain types, especially deer, venison and pheasants. Since the Norman Conquest, much energy has been devoted to protecting large areas of land as hunting preserves. The consumption of meat from wild birds and animals found on these lands was restricted to the aristocracy (hence the art of the poacher). This restriction made venison and game birds sought after as a food for grand meals and large feasts, having a far higher status than beef, mutton and pork.

Once upon a time, the category of game included a much wider range than that now available or eaten. They featured at great feasts, together with exotic domestic fowl such as peacocks. Birds that appeared on the table included herons, bustards, bittern, curlews, plover, and numerous small birds no longer considered as food in Britain.

Grouse are generally regarded as the finest game birds the British Isles have to offer, although this may in part be to do with the shooting as much as the eating. Thousands of acres of moorland are devoted to their welfare, producing a landscape that consists of a mosaic of heather plants of various ages (older growth to provide cover and nesting sites, young green shoots for the birds to feed on). An older name for grouse was moorcock, and recipes for this appear intermittently in early English cookery books. Real interest in them seems to have originated with the mid-19th century fashion for shooting on Highland estates and for things Scottish in general. The birds have given the English language the term 'the Glorious Twelfth', as their pursuit opens the shooting season on 12th August.

The good flavour of game birds were prized for stock-making in kitchens of the past. In the 18th century, partridges were often added to the general brew of meats for the rich gravies and meat coulis that seem to have flavoured or accompanied almost every meat at the table. In the

19th century, birds were often used as a basis for consommé. Older birds, unsuitable for presenting as roasts, were employed for such dishes. Methods for roasting, though, always seem to have been plain and unadorned.

The presentation of game birds at table has changed over the centuries. Our ancestors expected to find various extremities still in place. Tastes seem to have changed in the early 19th century: in a precursor of a sentiment now widespread, Eliza Acton commented that pheasant 'was formerly always sent to the table with the head on, but it was a barbarous custom, which has been partially abandoned of late in the best houses, and which it is hoped may soon be altogether superseded by one of better taste.'

Pheasants can be extremely cheap (especially if you live near a large shoot and can dress them yourself). This is because pheasant chicks are often hatched indoors and given extra feed after they are released into the woods, which has vastly increased their availability and decreased their price. Some game birds, however, remain very expensive – such as grouse, woodcock and snipe. They can also be expensive to buy. Game provides a range of flavours and textures outside the range of domestic birds, and meat that is very definitely free-range.

Buying Game

All birds intended for roasting should be young ones. You will have to trust the game dealer, and buy earlier in the season rather than later. Game from the wild (except pigeon and rabbit) is also subject to laws restricting the times of year when it can be shot. The seasons when wild birds are available are as follows:

• pheasant: 1 October–1 February
• partridge: 1 September–1 February
• grouse: 12 August–10 December
• mallard, teal, widgeon: 31 January–1 September
• woodcock: 1 October–31 March
• snipe: 12 August–31 January

Hanging game both develops the flavour and helps to tenderise the flesh. Birds are hung by the neck, complete with feathers and insides, in a cool, airy place. The length of time for which they should be hung depends on the weather (a longer time is required in cold weather) and is also, to some extent, a matter of taste. The old method of telling if a pheasant was sufficiently well hung was to try pulling one of the tail feathers: if it came out easily, the bird was judged to be at the correct stage. Some households took things to extremes, and people who had worked as kitchen staff in the late 19th and early 20th centuries would tell of pheasants hung until they were very 'high' indeed. Not nice for those who had to dress them, however ambrosial the flavour may have been considered. It is unlikely that a purchased pheasant would now be hung for more than 7–10 days, except by special request. Times for other birds differ: partridge and grouse need only 2–3 days. Hanging was also, in the days before freezing as a preservation method, a means of extending the season for game a little, as birds

Buying game is something of a lottery. If some game birds are now relatively inexpensive, this is partly because they are prepared quickly, in large numbers and with the aid of machines. This is understandable: plucking and eviscerating are not pleasant jobs, but if they are done carefully and neatly, the birds look nicer, and the skin will crisp better. Unless you can buy game birds freshly shot and in the feathers, and are willing and able to pluck and dress them yourself, then only trial and error will show who prepares them the best.

A pheasant will serve 4 people. Allow one grey-legged partridge per person; a red-legged one may be larger, but it is still probably safer to allow one per person. Though relatively large and meaty, allow one grouse per person. Wild duck varies in size according to species, but most of the meat is on the breast (in common with most waterfowl) and is on the shallow side. Allow one bird for 2 people.

Cooking Game Birds

The old expression relating to the cooking of small game birds and wild duck was that they 'should just fly through the kitchen'. Cookery books usually state that game birds, especially small ones such as partridge and grouse, should be served rare (with the breast meat pink or just done). This is not to everyone's taste, and can leave the legs quite underdone. If you wish to serve the birds whole then you may have to compromise: if you would like the legs to be cooked through, the breast meat will be more cooked with some risk of dryness; if you would like the breast meat to be just done, the legs may be very underdone. Resting the bird helps. Alternatively – although purists would frown on this – carve off the breasts from the birds after a short rest, return the birds to the oven for a few minutes, then carve the legs and serve piled up on a crouton.

When serving grouse, remember that only young birds are suitable for roasting, so it is best to acquire them early in the season. Their flavour is rich, and usually described as 'distinctive'; almost all cookery books advise that they should be served very rare, but the leg meat of grouse can be bitter when undercooked, and the heathery flavour overpowering. Both these characteristics diminish as the bird approaches the medium stage of done-ness. Unless you are certain that you like the taste, it can be better to cook until the leg meat is fully done.

Roasting Times and Temperatures
- Pheasants: start at 200°C, 400°F, Gas mark 6 for 20 minutes, then reduce to 180°C, 350°F, Gas mark 4 for 20–30 minutes. Don't overcook, as they become dry, tough and flavourless.
- Partridges: start at 200°C, 400°F, Gas mark 6 for 10 minutes, then reduce to 180°C, 350°F, Gas mark 4 for 10–15 minutes, or until done to taste. Partridges have a rich and distinctive flavour. There are two species available: the native grey-legged, and the slightly larger French red-legged partridge, a bird introduced to south-eastern England. Both make good eating, but they must be young for roasting, and the red-legged needs care to make sure it doesn't dry out.

- Grouse: start at 200°C, 400°F, Gas mark 6 for 10–15 minutes, then reduce to 180°C, 350°F, Gas mark 4 for 10–15 minutes.
- Wild ducks (teal, widgeon): start at 200°C, 400°F, Gas mark 6 for 10 minutes, then reduce to 180°C, 350°F, Gas mark 4 for 10–15 minutes.
- Mallard: start at 200°C, 400°F, Gas mark 6 for 15 minutes, then reduce to 180°C, 350°F, Gas mark 4 for about 25 minutes.

Roast Game Birds

Season the bird, or birds, inside and out with salt and pepper. Add a squeeze of lemon juice to the body cavity. Bard with bacon or spread butter over the breast. Do not cover. Put the birds on their backs in a roasting tin just large enough to hold them. Roast according to the times and temperatures given above.

About 10 minutes before the end of cooking, remove any covering from the breast of the birds, baste well and dust with flour to froth them (see page 13). When cooked to your liking (examine the colour of the flesh between the thigh and body of the bird to ascertain how well done they are), remove the birds to a hot serving dish and keep warm while you make the gravy.

Tip off as much fat as possible from the roasting tin. If the flour from frothing the birds hasn't fallen into the tin, add a tiny quantity to the residues – about 1 teaspoon – and stir it in over gentle heat to cook and brown slightly. Then stir in 250ml (9fl oz) well-flavoured chicken stock. Bring to the boil and cook gently for a few minutes. Check the seasoning. The gravy should be clear, thin and well flavoured.

Add a sprig of thyme to the body cavity of grouse, and serve them on toast, one piece per bird. Should you have the livers of the grouse, cook lightly in butter, then season and mash and spread over the toast before serving.

Making Stock from Game Bones

If all you have available is the leftovers from roasting a few partridge or a brace of grouse, it is still possible to make stock. Collect all the bones, skin and debris of the birds and put in a suitable pan. The remains of 4 partridge or 2 grouse will produce about 750ml (1¼ pints) of well-flavoured stock when finished. 3–4 tablespoons of sherry, port or wine will improve the stock – add it and heat till it boils, then add 1 litre (1¾ pints) of water. Also add a piece of onion; a few black peppercorns; a bouquet garni made of bay leaf, parsley stalks and thyme sprigs; a small carrot; and some ham trimmings if you have them. Simmer very gently for 1½–2 hours, topping up with fresh water if necessary, or use a slow cooker. Strain the stock, measure it and (if necessary) reduce by fast boiling. Venison or hare bones can be used in the same way.

Roast Woodcock or Snipe

It is unusual to see woodcock and snipe on sale, but if you know a keen shooter, or a game keeper, you might be able to get them. Allow one woodcock or two snipe per person. They should arrive with their insides intact (snipe will still have their heads on). This sounds gruesome, but the insides are considered good eating, although you will have to remove the gizzard.

4 woodcock or 8 snipe
4 slices of toast
unsalted butter
salt and freshly ground black pepper

Serves 4

With a small, sharp knife, make a small opening at the vent and insert your finger to remove the gizzard – it is a little round hard lump, like a very thick button. Pull it out, cut it off and discard it. Push any of the trail (the insides) that came out with it back into the bird.

Should you wish your snipe to be presented *à l'ancienne*, skin the heads, turn them back to the body and use the long bills to skewer the thick part of the thigh, through the body and out through the other thigh.

Place each bird on a slice of toast, season with a little salt and pepper, and roast in a hot oven, 220°C, 425°F, Gas mark 7, giving snipe about 10 minutes, and the slightly larger woodcock 15–20 minutes.

At the end of cooking, have ready very hot plates (or a hot serving dish). Remove the birds, lay the toasts on the hot plates, scoop out the remaining trail and mash with a little melted butter and seasoning; spread this over the toasts and replace a bird on each one. This is not as disgusting as it sounds to our delicate sensibilities; the trail tastes like strong liver pâté. Woodcock is thought to be the most delicious of game birds; the 19th-century gourmets considered thigh of woodcock to be the best bit.

Roast Pheasant with Pancetta and Lemon

This recipe is based on an aside by Anne Cobbett in The English Housekeeper *(1840). She remarked that the French laid slices of lemon over the pheasant breast and then covered it with bacon and wrapped the lot in paper. I have dispensed with the paper and used pancetta in this recipe because it is available in very thin slices, which create a thin, crisp crust round the bird. Bacon can be used instead, especially if you can buy fatty, old-fashioned dry-cured bacon cut very thin on a bacon slicer.*

1 pheasant
1 lemon
75g (3oz) pancetta, thinly sliced
unsalted butter

1 teaspoon plain flour
150ml (5fl oz) stock made
    from the giblets of the bird,
    or from chicken or veal

Serves 3–4

Skin the pheasant (add the skin to the stockpot). Preheat the oven to 200°C, 400°F, Gas mark 6.

Peel the lemon completely, This is most easily done by cutting off each end, then standing it up like a little barrel on a board, and slicing the peel off in vertical strips, taking off zest, skin and pith together. Cut the lemon across in the thinnest possible slices, removing any pips as you go.

Lay the pheasant on its back and cover the breast and as much as possible of the upper surface of the bird with the lemon slices. Then swaddle it up in pancetta, overlapping the slices where necessary. Take a piece of string, pass it under the back of the bird about halfway down the wings, then bring it up over the breast in a cross and back under in another cross somewhere near the middle of the thighs and finally up again, tying it neatly to keep the pancetta in place.

Lightly butter a roasting tin and put the pheasant in on its back. Roast, checking occasionally to make sure the pancetta or bacon isn't browning too much; if it is darkening a lot, turn the heat down slightly and roast for a little longer. After 20 minutes, reduce the heat to 180°C, 350°F, Gas mark 4 and roast for a further 20–30 minutes. Test for done-ness with a skewer pushed into the thickest part of the leg; if the juices run clear, or with only a slight hint of pink, it is done.

Remove the pheasant to a warmed serving dish and cut away the string. Pour the juices from the roasting tin into a small bowl and skim off as much fat as possible, returning about a dessertspoon of fat to the tin. Sprinkle in the flour, then stir in the juices and mix to a paste. Add the stock, bit by bit, stirring constantly and bring to the boil; you should have a thin, well-flavoured gravy.

Remove the pancetta (which should be deliciously crisp) just before carving and serve.

Salmi of Game

A salmi is a dish of game roasted very rare and allowed to cool, then marinated in a highly seasoned sauce in which it is gently reheated; this should be done in a bain-marie. The recipe can also be used for reheating leftover game that has been roasted rare – although, as Colonel Kenney-Herbert remarked, the result is really a hash. A dish whose origins go back a long way, it became a classic of 19th- and 20th-century English game cookery.

a brace of partridges or other
   suitable game (such a brace
   of grouse, or a pheasant)
75g (3oz) ham
100g (4oz) onion, peeled and finely
   chopped
50g (2oz) carrot finely chopped
15g (½oz) celery finely chopped
1 teaspoon fresh thyme
1 teaspoon fresh marjoram
1 teaspoon fresh rosemary
½ teaspoon black pepper

¼ teaspoon salt
300ml (10fl oz) light stock or water
30g (1oz) unsalted butter
30g (1oz) plain flour
100g (4oz) button mushrooms, cooked
   in unsalted butter
1 tablespoon lemon or orange juice

TO SERVE
triangular croutons of bread fried in
   unsalted butter, or hot, crisp toast
lemon or orange quarters, to garnish

Serves 2–3

Roast the birds in a hot oven, 220°C, 425°F, Gas mark 7 for 10–15 minutes, or until nicely coloured. Remove and allow to cool. Cut off the breasts and legs, remove the skin and any fat, trim neatly, and put the meat in a cool place.

Put the skin and trimmings from the birds in a pan. Break up the bones and add them too, along with the ham, chopped vegetables, herbs, salt and pepper. Cover with the stock and simmer for 1 hour, adding a little more stock or water if the liquid seems to be evaporating too much. Then pour the contents through a sieve into a bowl. Press the debris in the sieve with the back of a wooden spoon to extract as much broth as possible, but don't rub any solids through (discard these).

Melt the butter in a clean pan and add the flour to make a roux. Allow it to cook gently for a few minutes until it turns a light brown. Then stir in the broth to make a smooth sauce. Taste, and add a little more salt if necessary. Add the mushrooms, lemon juice and the pieces of game. Heat very gently – barely simmer – until the game is thoroughly hot.

Serve the game pieces in a warmed dish with the croutons or toast tucked round and the lemon or orange to garnish, and hand the sauce separately.

Orange Sauce for Wild Duck

This is based on a mid-19th-century recipe by Anne Cobbett; it isn't clear which type of orange she used, but the bitter–sour flavour of Seville orange is better with this close-textured, gamey meat than sweet oranges, and makes a good midwinter combination. If you have to use sweet oranges, add a little bitter orange marmalade at the end. The 'bite' of the hot pepper is surprising, but very good with the duck.

Roast the duck following the general method for game birds (see page 115). While the duck is roasting, make the sauce.

30g (1oz) unsalted butter
zest of 1 Seville orange, cut in fine strips
   and blanched in boiling water
a pinch of cayenne pepper, to taste
juice of 1 lemon
salt
sugar

Serves 2

Melt the butter in a small pan and add the orange zest, cayenne pepper and lemon juice. Bring to the boil and cook for a minute to reduce slightly. Taste, and add a pinch of salt and a little sugar until the bitter/sweet balance of the sauce is pleasing.

If Seville oranges are unavailable, use a sweet orange and a little bitter marmalade, omitting the sugar.

Salad of Game

Another Victorian recipe inspired by Alexis Soyer. The essential elements are salad leaves, the game and the sauce, producing a remarkably pretty, high Victorian result. The sauce should be made principally with cream as he suggests; don't be tempted to turn it into a mayonnaise by replacing the cream with olive oil.

a brace of roast grouse, or partridge,
   or a pheasant, cold
salad leaves in season – watercress
   would have been the 19th-century
   choice, but use whatever appeals
   (though not iceberg lettuce)

FOR THE SAUCE
1 medium egg yolk
1 small shallot, peeled and
   very finely chopped
1 teaspoon finely chopped
   fresh parsley
1 teaspoon finely chopped
   fresh tarragon

1 teaspoon finely chopped
   fresh chervil
a small piece of fresh green
   chilli, finely chopped
1 tablespoon white wine vinegar
2 tablespoons mild olive oil
125ml (4fl oz) double cream
salt

FOR THE GARNISH
6–8 eggs, hard-boiled
unsalted butter, softened
2–3 anchovy fillets in oil, drained
1–2 gherkins, sliced
sprigs of chervil or tarragon

Serves 4–6

If you wish to serve this decorated in true 19th-century style, choose a shallow dish with a wide rim, and have a little softened butter ready. To make the sauce, put the egg yolk in a bowl and add the shallot, herbs, chilli and vinegar. Drizzle in the olive oil, stirring well. Season with salt. Whip the cream until very thick and stir into the mixture. Chill.

Carve the meat off the birds. Skin, trim and divide into neat pieces. Arrange the salad leaves on the serving dish and top with the meat. Pour on the sauce.

To make the garnish, peel the eggs and cut them in quarters lengthways. Arrange them around the rim of the dish, using a dab of softened butter under each piece to prevent it sliding around. Cut diamond shapes from the anchovy fillets and sliced gherkins, and use them to make a border round the edge. Add the herb sprigs as a final flourish.

Right: Salad of Game.
Next page: Wild Duck with Orange Sauce.

Fried Breadcrumbs

A classic British accompaniment for game, in use since at least the 19th century.

15g (½oz) unsalted butter
50g (2oz) breadcrumbs, made from stale white bread

Serves 4

Melt the butter in a small frying pan. Don't let it burn. Add the breadcrumbs and fry
gently, stirring frequently, for 5–10 minutes, or until the crumbs are crisp and golden.

Game Chips

*These need maincrop potatoes, preferably ones that are long and quite regular in shape;
Maris Piper are a variety that work reasonably well. It is difficult to recommend how
many to use, as most people will eat as many game chips as you care to put in front of
them, or until you get fed up with deep frying.*

You will also need oil or fat (beef dripping is best) for deep frying, and sea salt.

Peel the potatoes and trim off any obviously irregular edges. Cut to give very narrow strips, about
2mm (⅟₁₆in) thick and the same wide, and as long as the potatoes allow. Drop them into a bowl
of cold water and leave to soak for about 15 minutes.

When you are ready to cook, drain them and spread on a cloth or kitchen paper and dry
them thoroughly (this is important, otherwise they will make the hot oil spit viciously).

Heat the oil in a deep-fat fryer. The recommended temperature on a frying thermometer is
180–185°C (350–360°F). Alternatively, drop a small cube of bread into the hot fat and observe
how long it takes to brown; if it rises to the surface and browns in 30 seconds, the fat is hot enough
(don't let it get to smoking point, which is too hot).

When the fat is hot enough, fry the chips in batches – don't overcrowd the pan. Cook briskly
until golden, then remove with a slotted spoon and drain well on kitchen paper.

Sprinkle with salt – a flaky one such as Maldon looks nice – and serve.

Left: Game Chips.
Previous page: Croquettes of Game.

Leftovers

Croquettes of Game

A croquette should be small, dainty and, as the derivation of the word from the French croquant suggests, crunchy. They became a favourite 19th-century method for converting leftovers (of any meat) into something quite different through the medium of frying. It was a time when richness and elaboration in food were admired, and a substantial girth indicated wealth, and also plenty of servants to do the cooking. Serve with salad for lunch or as appetisers.

180g (6oz) cold roast pheasant
50g (2oz) cooked ham,
   including some of the fat
2 medium mushrooms,
   sautéed in a little unsalted butter
10g (¼oz) unsalted butter
10g (¼oz) plain flour
150ml (5fl oz) stock
1 tablespoon medium sherry
a pinch of thyme

a squeeze of lemon juice
1 teaspoon redcurrant jelly
salt and pepper
oil or fat, for deep frying

FOR THE COATING
2 medium eggs
about 300g (10½oz) fine white
   breadcrumbs made from
   stale bread

Makes 16–18 croquettes

Mince the game meat, ham and mushrooms together. Melt the butter in a small pan, stir in the flour, and make a sauce with the stock. Add the minced meat mixture, sherry and a little thyme. Cook over low heat for a few minutes, stirring well. The mixture should have the consistency of jam. Season to taste with a little lemon juice, redcurrant jelly, and salt and pepper. Pour the mixture into a shallow plate or on to a tray and allow it to go completely cold.

Start the egg-and-breadcrumb process about 1 hour before you want to cook the croquettes. Beat the eggs in a soup dish or other shallow bowl. Put the breadcrumbs in another bowl.

Take the cold meat mixture and divide into portions – this should make about 18, each the size of a small egg. Pass them through the beaten egg, then through the breadcrumbs, and leave for 30 minutes to dry. Repeat the process, and leave to dry for a little while.

Heat the oil in a deep-fat fryer to 175–180°C, 347–350°F. Deep-fry the croquettes until golden brown and thoroughly hot all the way through. Drain on kitchen paper and serve immediately.

Game and Lentil Soup

A soup-stew for a winter's day.

2 tablespoons olive oil
100g (4oz) unsmoked bacon or
    pancetta, cut in 5mm (¼in) cubes
1 medium onion, peeled and chopped
1 garlic clove, peeled and crushed
½ a small celeriac, peeled and cut
    in 5mm (¼in) cubes
2 small–medium potatoes, peeled and
    cut in 5mm (¼in) cubes
1 small fresh rosemary sprig
6 fresh thyme sprigs
100g (4oz) green lentils

1–1½ litres (1¾–2¾ pints) game stock
    (see page 115)
any leftover meat from the roast birds
    or scraps picked from the carcasses,
    cut into small pieces
salt and pepper

TO SERVE
fresh parsley, chopped
1 small garlic clove, peeled and chopped
breadcrumbs or croutons fried
    in unsalted butter

Serves 4

Heat the oil in a large saucepan. Add the bacon, onion and garlic. Cook briskly for a few minutes, stirring all the time, until the onion begins to turn golden. Add the celeriac, potatoes and herbs and cook a little longer, then add the lentils and pour in the stock. Bring to the boil, add any meat scraps and simmer gently for about 30 minutes. Check that the lentils are soft (cook a little longer if necessary). Taste and adjust the seasoning.

To serve, divide between 4 large bowls and top with a little parsley chopped together with garlic, or some breadcrumbs or croutons.

Rabbit and Hare

Rabbits are not native to the British Isles, something that may seem surprising when one considers how they breed in our countryside – like, well, rabbits. Formerly they were considered a delicacy, carefully nurtured in warrens; then they escaped and became pests. In the 19th century, they were the only wild meat available to the rural poor, although even taking rabbits was sometimes regarded as poaching. Hares are native, and they and the rabbit population occupy roughly the same ecological niche, although the two species seem to have a slightly uneasy balance as to which dominates in the countryside.

Rabbit and hare meat was noted for its leanness and dryness and in the past was usually larded. The heads were left on (but skinned) for roasting. A hare was usually stuffed with forcemeat, with the head set upright and the ears propped so they stood erect, a custom that must have provided endless trouble for the person tending the spit. Illustrations from 18th- and 19th-century cookery books show how they should be served, looking a little astonished by the whole thing. Both hares and rabbits sometimes had their body cavities lined with streaky bacon before cooking. The juices from roast hare tend to curdle during cooking, and an initial basting of milk or cream was often recommended 'to draw away the blood', the sauce being made with butter, claret and gravy from some other animal.

Most rabbits sold in Britain are wild ones and their roasting qualities are uncertain. Active lives can be reflected in lean, dry meat and an excessively rabbity flavour. Treat them gently: marinades are useful for counteracting dryness and adding flavour; stuffing or barding also adds fat and flavour. They need to be well cooked. Wild rabbits weigh from 500g (1lb 2oz) to 1kg (2¼lb); the heavier ones will be about right for 4 people). Most of the meat is in the hind legs and the saddle, as the forequarter contains too much bone to be really rewarding. The creature will usually arrive skinned and paunched (unless you have shot it yourself) but should still contain the 'pluck' – the kidneys, liver, lungs and heart. Discard the lungs. The liver and kidneys are delicacies, and can be incorporated into a stuffing mixture or used to make stock or sauce. Note that farmed rabbits are usually imported, some from very intensive systems.

Hares should not be confused with rabbits, least of all in the kitchen. Hares are bigger, meatier, with dark flesh and a rich, strong flavour. They are seasonal, like game birds, and are available from August to March.

A hare should hang for about 1 week. Only young ones (leverets) are tender enough for roasting, so you need to be able to trust your game dealer or butcher about this. A hare will also have the pluck in place, and sometimes be accompanied by a little container with the blood of the animal (used for thickening moist-cooked dishes such as jugged hare, but not in roasting). Remove the pluck; use the liver in stuffing, and the rest in stock. Hare should be well cooked, and if roasted whole, the forelegs should be drawn back and the hind legs forwards and held in place with skewers through the body (the sinews under the legs need to be cut to achieve this).

A whole hare will weigh 2–2.5kg (4½–5lb), and feed 6 people easily. They are sometimes divided into forequarters and a joint comprising the saddle and hindquarters: count the ribs forwards from the back, and cut after the sixth rib (use the forequarters for a different, slow-cooked moist dish, such as soup or jugged hare). For a small, neat joint of the saddle only, remove the hind legs with slanting cuts across them, from the tail to where the thigh joins the side of the body. A heavy cleaver will be needed to cut through the backbone, so you may prefer to persuade the butcher to joint the animal.

Hare responds well to marinating, and can be left for 2–3 days in a marinade, either in a cold place or in the refrigerator. It is still a good idea to lard it, and using lardons rolled in a seasoning mixture takes both fat and flavour deep into the meat. Should you lack the wherewithal or time to lard, then bard with a few pieces of bacon instead. Use very thinly sliced, very streaky bacon for barding (this needs to be cut using an old-fashioned bacon slicer). If you can't obtain this, it is better to use pancetta than a chunkily sliced ordinary bacon. Whichever you choose, it should be unsmoked.

Redcurrant jelly or other fruit jellies, such as quince or rowanberry, make excellent accompaniments for hare.

Carving Rabbit and Hare

The best meat in both hares and rabbits is in the saddle, the muscles lying on either side of and parallel to the backbone. Carve this in long thin slices. Smaller slices can be cut from the hind legs. The shoulders, which according to Eliza Acton 'are not much esteemed though sometimes liked by sportsmen', should be taken off by dividing the joint from the ribs.

Rabbit with Verjuice Gravy

A simple marinade using verjuice (see also page 27). It is a good flavouring for rabbit. If you can't get verjuice, use cider mixed with a little cider vinegar in this recipe. The rabbit can be stuffed with the mixture shown opposite; if you wish to do this, add the stuffing after marinating.

125ml (4fl oz) verjuice
3 tablespoons olive oil
1 rabbit
freshly ground black pepper
100g (4oz) unsmoked bacon or pancetta,
    thinly sliced
salt (optional)

Serves 4

Mix the verjuice, olive oil and a grind of pepper in a deep glass or china bowl. Put the rabbit into this mixture and let it marinate for 2–3 hours, turning occasionally.

Preheat the oven to 150°C, 300°F, Gas mark 2. When ready to cook, take the rabbit out of the marinade (reserve this) and wrap it in bacon. Place it in a roasting tin or dish in which it fits quite snugly and roast gently for about 1 hour. Then pour the marinade round it and continue to cook gently for another 30–45 minutes, by which time the meat should be cooked but not dried out. Keep an eye on it, and if the juices show signs of drying up and catching, add a little water.

Remove the rabbit to a warm serving dish. A relatively small amount of concentrated, nicely coloured juice should remain in the cooking dish. Make sure that you scrape any browned bits off the sides of the dish into this gravy. Then skim off any excess fat, taste to check the seasoning (the bacon may have provided enough salt) and serve alongside the rabbit.

Stuffing for Rabbit

Lemon and herb flavours are very typical of 18th- and 19th-century recipes for stuffing all sorts of meat. This is based on a 19th-century recipe, given by Anne Cobbett in The English Housekeeper *(1840).*

50g (2oz) fresh white breadcrumbs
2–3 large fresh parsley sprigs, finely chopped
3 shallots, peeled and finely chopped
zest of ½ lemon (preferably unwaxed), grated
freshly grated nutmeg
freshly ground black pepper
1 medium egg yolk
about 2 tablespoons double cream
½ teaspoon salt

Makes enough to stuff a small rabbit

Mix the breadcrumbs, parsley, shallots, lemon zest and salt. Season generously with grated nutmeg and freshly ground pepper, then bind with the egg yolk and cream. Use this mixture to stuff the body of the rabbit, sewing the flaps of skin over to hold it.

Two Sauces for Roast Rabbit

The first of these appears to have been a standard English accompaniment for roast rabbit in the 18th century. The second was quoted by Robert May, in the late 17th century, as a list of flavourings, 'in the French fashion'.

Liver and Parsley Sauce

the liver of the rabbit
1 small bunch of curly parsley, stems removed
50g (2oz) unsalted butter
salt

Serves 4

Simmer the rabbit liver very gently in a little water until it is just cooked – this will take only a few minutes. Drain, then chop finely.

Put the parsley in a small bowl and pour boiling water over it. Drain this and chop finely as well.

Melt the butter very gently and stir in the liver and parsley. Check the seasoning and add a little salt if necessary.

Onion and Mustard Sauce

30g (1oz) unsalted butter
1 small–medium onion, peeled and finely sliced
1 dessertspoon Dijon mustard
lemon juice

Serves 4

Melt the butter in a small pan and cook the onion gently until translucent (don't let it brown). Stir in the mustard and thin the sauce with a little lemon juice.

Right: Two Sauces for Roast Rabbit.

Roast Rabbit with Apple

Rabbit responds well to the apple and cream treatment more usually associated with pheasant.

3–4 tablespoons Calvados or whisky
1–2 tablespoons cider vinegar
the leaves from a few fresh thyme sprigs
4–5 juniper berries, crushed
1 rabbit
1–2 aromatic dessert apples
bacon fat, butter or olive oil
150ml (5fl oz) double cream
salt and pepper

Serves 4

Mix the Calvados, cider vinegar, thyme and juniper berries in a deep glass or china bowl. Put the rabbit into this mixture and let it marinate for 2–3 hours.

Preheat the oven to 150°C, 300°F, Gas mark 2.

When ready to cook, peel and core the apples and cut them into small chunks. Take the rabbit out of the marinade and stuff the body cavity with apples. Grease the roasting tin and put the rabbit in (bard the meat if desired, although this is not strictly necessary). Add the marinade, and cover with foil. Roast gently for about 1–1½ hours; check to make sure the juices don't catch and add a little water or light stock if necessary.

When the rabbit is cooked, remove it to a warmed serving dish. There should be a small amount of concentrated juice left in the roasting tin (boil to reduce it to a few syrupy tablespoons if it seems on the liquid side). Add the cream and bring back to the boil; the sauce should be quite thick. Taste and adjust the seasoning.

Left: Roast Rabbit with Apple.

Roast Hare

It is not strictly necessary to marinate a hare before roasting, but the meat does respond well to it.

FOR THE MARINADE
4 shallots, peeled and chopped
1 carrot, peeled, halved lengthways and cut in slices
1 bay leaf
4 tablespoons brandy
1 garlic clove, peeled and crushed
1 tablespoon roughly chopped fresh parsley
a few fresh thyme sprigs
a few black peppercorns, crushed
1 tablespoon olive oil
1 dessertspoon balsamic vinegar

To marinate 1 hare

Mix all the ingredients for the marinade together. Put the hare in a glass, pottery, plastic or stainless steel bowl and pour over the marinade. Leave for at least 6 hours or up to 3 days, turning the meat occasionally in the mixture.

Remove the hare from the marinade, then stuff if desired (see recipe on page 132). Stitch the flaps together to hold the mixture and skewer the legs in place. Wrap the animal in bacon or pork fat and roast at 170°C, 325°F, Gas mark 3 for 15 minutes then reduce the heat to 220°C, 425°F, Gas mark 7 and roast for another 40–60 minutes. Discard the juices from roasting, as they will contain the blood of the hare and curdle any gravy made with them.

Serve with Potatoes Roast in Double Cream and with Herbs (see page 150) and redcurrant jelly.

Saddle of Hare with Cream Sauce

1 saddle of hare
unsalted butter or olive oil
1 carrot, peeled
½ medium onion, peeled
1 garlic clove, peeled
milk
200ml (7fl oz) beer
salt
a little stock, preferably game
150ml (5fl oz) double cream

FOR LARDING
6 black peppercorns
2 cloves
the leaves from 2-3 fresh thyme sprigs
nutmeg
50g (2oz) pork back fat in a piece

Serves 2-3

First, for the larding, grind the peppercorns and cloves to a powder with the thyme leaves. Grate in a little nutmeg and mix well. Cut the back fat into neat lardons, 3–4cm (1¼–1½in) long and a little less than 5mm (¼in) in section. Roll them in the spice mixture and use them to lard the saddle as neatly as you can, drawing them into the meat at roughly 2cm (¾in) intervals, at right angles to the backbone. This can be done a few hours in advance and the saddle left in a cool place until needed. Alternatively, bard with a few rashers of bacon.

Preheat the oven to 220°C, 425°F, Gas mark 7.

When ready to cook, grease a small roasting tin lightly with butter or olive oil. Take the carrot and onions and cut them into rough chunks. Arrange them in the roasting tin, push the garlic clove in among them, and sit the saddle on top, larded side up. Sprinkle with salt.

Put the hare in the oven and cook for 10 minutes. Baste a couple of times with a little milk. Then turn the heat down to 180°C, 350°F, Gas mark 4 and continue cooking for another 15–20 minutes. Halfway through this time, discard the milk and any juices in the roasting tin and pour over the beer. Baste again a couple of times as cooking progresses.

When just cooked through (test by piercing the meat at the thickest part with a skewer; if the juices run clear or with just a hint of pink, it is done), remove the saddle to a warm serving dish and allow it to rest. Pour the beery cooking juices into a pan and skim off any fat. Add the cream and boil until only a few tablespoons remain. Taste and adjust the seasoning.

Stuffing for Roast Hare

This is enough for one hare (marinated first, if desired). See the recipe on page 130 for roasting instructions.

125g (4½oz) slightly stale bread, torn into small pieces
½ small onion, peeled and finely chopped
the leaves stripped from 6 fresh thyme sprigs
1 tablespoon finely chopped fresh parsley
2 anchovy fillets, chopped (if using salted ones, rinse well)
grated zest of ½ lemon (preferably unwaxed)
a generous pinch of nutmeg
a pinch of salt
freshly ground black pepper
stock or milk, to moisten
the pluck – heart, liver and kidneys of the hare
a little butter, for frying
30g (1oz) unsalted butter, melted

Serves 4–6

Mix together all the ingredients except the stock and pluck, then use just enough of the liquid to moisten the mixture. Sauté the liver, kidneys and heart lightly in the butter, then chop and add to the stuffing mixture.

Leftovers

Hare Sauce for Pappardelle

Historically, leftover roast hare would have been hashed just as most other meats were in British cookery, and presented with sippets of toast, croutons of fried bread, or possibly in a timbale of macaroni, the cooked pasta used to line a mould with the hashed meat as a filling. Today, the hare is more likely to be used for a pasta sauce in which the rich flavour of hare means a little goes a long way.

olive oil
1–2 rashers unsmoked bacon, finely chopped
1 shallot, or ½ small onion, peeled and finely chopped
1 garlic clove, peeled and finely chopped
150g (5oz) cooked hare (not bits from the outside hardened by cooking, or sinew), minced
2 cloves, ground to powder

50ml (2fl oz) Marsala or Madeira wine
150–200ml (5–7fl oz) stock from the bones of the hare
chopped fresh parsley
salt and pepper

TO SERVE
about 450g (1lb) fresh pappardelle pasta
a little unsalted butter, melted
grated Parmesan

Serves 4

Heat a little oil in a frying pan and cook the bacon, shallot and garlic gently, stirring frequently, until the shallot begins to turn golden. Add the hare, the cloves and a grind of pepper. Pour in the Marsala and let it boil away to almost nothing. Add the stock and parsley, and bring to the boil, then turn the heat down. Leave to simmer very gently for 1 hour (or more if you have time). Check occasionally to make sure there is some liquid left, but towards the end of the cooking time allow most of it to evaporate; this sauce should be fairly dry. Taste for seasoning and add a little salt if necessary.

To serve, stir into bowls of pappardelle that has been cooked, drained and dressed with a little butter. Serve with a bowl of grated Parmesan cheese.

Venison

'Venison' once meant the flesh of any wild mammal hunted for food, and so technically would have included hare and animals such as wild boar. It has now come to apply specifically to the meat of deer. The right to hunt these animals was a jealously guarded privilege of the aristocracy in the past, and few ordinary people tasted the meat, unless it was poached.

Deer prefer woodland habitats generally, but red deer, the largest, are now mostly found in the Scottish Highlands. Roe deer are found in woodland all over Britain. Fallow deer, also widespread, are probably a species introduced in the distant past, but seem to have been firmly established by the time of the Norman Conquest. All were much valued for meat by our ancestors.

Venison was a mark of status, and there were many attempts to imitate it by marinating beef and mutton. The meat tends to dryness, and the real thing was often larded, wrapped in paper and then enclosed in a 'huff' paste – a coarse pastry made of plain flour and water, sometimes with a little beef suet – before putting it to roast in front of an open fire. A sweet-sour sauce of venison gravy, port wine and a little sugar was served with it in the 18th century. Keeping venison well was a great preoccupation, and early cookery books include instructions for how to keep the flies off and prevent it tainting, usually by rubbing with black pepper and ginger, or what to do if the meat has already begun to go off.

The 19th-century fashion for things Scottish led to the development of deer stalking as a 'sport', and also saw the introduction of smaller species of deer, including sika and muntjac, mostly as ornamental animals in the parkland of country estates.

Two factors have made venison more accessible since the 1980s. One is the development of deer farming in this country, from small beginnings in the 1960s. The other is an increase in population among various deer species, especially red deer in the Scottish Highlands and roe deer in southern England. Farmed red deer venison is the most easily available, sold through supermarkets, butchers and by direct marketing, but wild red deer venison also reaches the market. For this, try a specialist game dealer, who may also be able to provide roe, fallow and even some of the smaller, more exotic species such as sika.

Deer farming does not involve complete domestication of the animals and they feed principally on grass. In terms of welfare, the meat is raised to high standards. Red deer venison should be hung for 2 weeks, as venison bought from a deer farm almost certainly will have been. Wild red deer venison will be leaner and less predictable in quality, but provided it has been carefully stalked and hung, it should be excellent. If you have the choice, buck venison is considered finer than doe. Venison generally is a dark red, fine-grained meat, which is very lean and low in saturated fat.

Cuts for roasting are the same from all deer but vary greatly in size according to species. Those from red deer are largest; a saddle from this animal will be too large for many domestic ovens and is usually split down the backbone and divided into loin and best end. Saddles from smaller species are left whole. The haunch (hind leg) is also a prime cut. These joints are best slightly underdone. Shoulder makes a good slow roast or pot roast.

Marinating, often recommended for venison, may have become popular because it acted as a short-term preservation method in the past. Whether to use a marinade or not is up to the individual; if you want to do so, a recipe is on page 136. Venison has the potential to be extremely dry when roasted: larding repays the effort required.

Carving venison from the smaller species is similar to carving mutton or lamb, although saddle or loin of red deer should be carved like sirloin. Cookery authors in the past were very insistent that venison shouldn't be allowed to get cold, and must be served on very hot plates. French beans were considered the best vegetable to go with it.

Redcurrant jelly is a traditional accompaniment for roast venison, but other fruit jellies, such as gooseberry or sloe, go well too. A jelly made from Japonica quince goes best of all, but you may have to make this yourself, unless you are lucky enough to find some on a Women's Institute stall or in a farmers' market.

Marinade for Venison

The quantities given here make enough to marinate a small joint, such as a haunch of roe deer.

2 tablespoons olive oil
40g (1½oz) carrot, scrubbed and finely chopped
50g (2oz) onion, peeled and finely chopped
½ celery stick, washed and finely chopped
1 garlic clove, peeled and crushed
10 black peppercorns, crushed
6 cloves, bruised
10 juniper berries, bruised
the leaves stripped off 4–6 fresh rosemary sprigs
6–8 fresh thyme sprigs
6 fresh marjoram sprigs
a handful of fresh parsley, chopped
4 bay leaves, the central spine cut out, chopped
½ teaspoon salt
the leaves from 2 large basil sprigs, torn into pieces
1 bottle good-quality red wine
4 tablespoons red wine vinegar

Makes 850ml (1½ pints)

Put the olive oil into a stainless steel or otherwise non-reactive pan and heat. Add all the ingredients except the basil, wine and vinegar, and fry, fairly briskly. Stir frequently and cook until the pieces of vegetable are beginning to catch and brown a little. Add the basil, wine and vinegar, and bring to the boil. Turn the heat very low and simmer gently for about 30 minutes.

Allow to cool completely before using. A piece of venison can be marinated in this mixture for 3–4 days, providing it is kept in a cool place or in the refrigerator, and turned a couple of times a day in the marinade. When ready to cook, remove the meat from the mixture, scraping off any bits of vegetable or herb clinging to it, and dry thoroughly.

This mixture can be re-used, but must be boiled first. If not used immediately, it should be frozen when cool.

Haunch of Roe Deer Venison

A treat for a small dinner party. This recipe is based on one by the Scottish cookery writer Mrs Cleland, whose book A New and Easy Method of Cookery *was first published in 1755. It uses the old method of wrapping the joint before roasting. It is not strictly necessary to either marinate or lard the meat, but it will be better for both.*

a leg of roe deer venison, 1.5–2 kg (3½–4½lb)
100g (4oz) pork back fat, or fatty unsmoked bacon, cut
    into strips 5mm (¼in) in section and 3cm (1¼in) long
unsalted butter
4–6 tablespoons sloe gin (or use stock and 2–3 juniper berries)
1 tablespoon plain flour and 1 tablespoon unsalted butter worked
    together to make a paste
salt and pepper

Serves 6

Marinate the venison (see page 136) for 24 hours if desired.

Preheat the oven to 230°C, 450°F, Gas mark 8. Remove the meat from the marinade, then dry it well. Lard with the back fat in neat rows (see page 12). Season with salt and pepper. Butter a large sheet of greaseproof paper (don't use foil), wrap the meat in it and tie with string like a parcel. Put on a rack in a roasting tin, and add a little water to the tin.

Roast for 20 minutes, then reduce the heat to 180°C, 350°F, Gas mark 4 and roast for another 1 hour. Some juice will drip through the paper into the tin. Add a little more water to the tin if the juices evaporate and show signs of catching. Remove the paper and allow the venison to cook for a further 10 minutes. The juices should run fairly pink at this stage, but the meat should be just cooked through and not dry. Venison can be served quite pink if you like meat that way, so use your own judgement and personal taste.

Put the venison on a hot plate to rest. Deglaze the roasting tin with the sloe gin (or stock, adding the juniper berries), and skim as much fat as possible from the surface of the juices. Put in a small pan and bring to the boil, then taste for seasoning, adding salt or pepper if desired. Reduce the heat to barely simmering and thicken with the flour and butter mixture, dropped in small pieces and stirred through the mixture until it thickens.

Best End of Red Deer Venison with Port and Redcurrant Jelly

A French-trimmed best end of red deer is an expensive joint, but is delicious and easy to cook. The sauce here recalls red wine sauces (port or claret) mixed with redcurrant jelly which were served in the 18th and 19th centuries, and the breadcrumb coating. It provides a pleasing contrast to the meat.

This roast is also good cold, although I would suggest cooking it on the same day as you wish to eat it, 5–6 hours beforehand. One best end of seven or so chops will serve 4, but don't expect leftovers. For two best ends, double everything except the quantity of marinade and the cooking times (which will remain the same). It is not essential to marinate this, but if doing so, leave for 2–3 days in the marinade.

1 best end of red deer venison, chined, backbone removed, the ends of the chop bones scraped bare
olive oil
salt
30g (1oz) dry breadcrumbs

30g (1oz) finely grated Parmesan
¼ teaspoon allspice
freshly ground black pepper

FOR THE SAUCE
100ml (3½fl oz) port
3 tablespoons redcurrant jelly

Serves 4

Preheat the oven to 230°C, 450°F, Gas mark 8. Put 2–3 tablespoons olive oil in a roasting tin. Rub another 1 tablespoon oil into the meat. Salt it lightly and place, with the bones downwards, in the tin. Roast for 15–20 minutes.

While it cooks, combine the breadcrumbs, Parmesan, allspice and a generous grind of black pepper. Remove the meat from the oven, baste, and then pour the oil from the tin into the bowl with the crumbs. Mix well, adding a little more oil if it looks dry (it shouldn't be too oily, but there should be enough to help the crumbs cling together a little). Press the crumbs gently over the upper surface of the meat; some will fall into the tin, but try to avoid this as much as possible.

Turn the heat down to 180°C, 350°F, Gas mark 4 and roast for another 20–30 minutes, or until done to the point you prefer. Remove the joint to a hot plate and keep in a warm place.

To make the sauce, add the port to the roasting tin and stir with a wooden spoon to scrape up the cooking residues. Strain into a small pan and add the redcurrant jelly. Heat, stirring all the time to help the jelly melt, until simmering. Check for seasoning.

Carve by cutting down between each chop and serve on hot plates. Serve the sauce separately.

Pot-roast Shoulder of Venison

about 100g (4oz) unsmoked bacon
 or pancetta in a single thick slice
1 teaspoon black peppercorns
3 cloves
¼ nutmeg, grated
1kg (2¼lb) boned shoulder of venison
250ml (9fl oz) white wine
2 tablespoons verjuice (optional,
 see page 27)
4 fresh bay leaves, bruised
1 bouquet garni – fresh marjoram,
 thyme, rosemary, a slice of lemon
 and a few bruised juniper berries,
 wrapped muslin, tied

oil or dripping
2 medium carrots, scraped and
 cut into chunks
½ medium onion, peeled and cut
 into 4 chunks
¼ medium turnip, peeled and
 cut into chunks

TO FINISH THE SAUCE
15g (½oz) butter and 15g (½oz) plain
 flour worked together to a paste
1 tablespoon salted capers,
 rinsed and roughly chopped
salt

Serves 6–8

Cut the bacon across into lardons, strips about 5mm (¼in) by 5mm (¼in) in section. Grind the peppercorns and cloves together and mix with the nutmeg. Spread this mixture on a plate and roll the lardons in it. Then use them to lard the venison from the inside at regular intervals, pulling them into the meat until they are just short of the outer surface (see page 12). Roll and tie the venison into a neat shape. Mix the white wine, verjuice and bay leaves in a glass bowl and add the venison and bouquet garni. Leave for about 3 hours, turning from time to time.

When you come to cook the meat, heat the oven to 140°C, 275°F, Gas mark 1. Heat a little oil in a casserole. When hot, add the carrots, onion and turnip, and fry until they begin to brown. Strain in the marinade and allow it to come to the boil. Add the venison and bouquet garni and cover the pot. Put in the oven and cook for about 3 hours, turning the meat occasionally.

At the end of this time, the venison should feel very tender when tested with a carving fork. Remove the meat to a warmed plate and discard the vegetables and bouquet garni. Boil the cooking juices fast until reduced to about half the original volume. Then move the pan off the heat and drop in the butter and flour mixture in little bits, shaking the pan to mix it in. This should thicken the sauce a little. Add the capers, check the seasoning and add salt if necessary.

Serve, handing round redcurrant jelly along with the meat and sauce. The meat around the lardons will appear pink or red – this is due to the saltpetre in the bacon cure, which leaches into the venison, making it a similar colour to cooked bacon.

Poivrade Sauce

*This was a classic accompaniment for venison in the late 19th and early 20th centuries.
Where it came from is unclear. Recipes vary quite significantly in detail, but always aimed for
a highly flavoured result. The consistent feature is a flavouring base of onions or shallots cooked
in an acid medium, such as lemon juice or wine vinegar. Serve with a plainly roast joint.*

10–15g (¼–½oz) unsalted butter
30g (1oz) ham or unsmoked
   bacon, chopped
1–2 shallots, about 60g (2½oz) in
   total, peeled and finely chopped
a piece of carrot 2–3cm (¾–1¼in)
   long, chopped
1 small slice of turnip, chopped
½ celery stick, chopped
a pinch of fresh thyme
1 fresh bay leaf
juice of 1 lemon

200ml (7fl oz) red wine
4 anchovy fillets, chopped
freshly ground black pepper
cayenne pepper

TO FINISH THE SAUCE
1 tablespoon unsalted butter
1 tablespoon plain flour
250ml (9fl oz) well-flavoured
   stock (beef for preference)
1 teaspoon redcurrant jelly
   or a pinch of sugar

Serves 4–6

Melt the butter in a saucepan and add the ham. Cook gently until the fat turns translucent. Add the
shallots and other vegetables, then turn up the heat and fry briskly together, stirring frequently, until
the vegetables begin to brown. Add the thyme, bay leaf and lemon juice, and allow the mixture to
bubble until the liquid has reduced to almost nothing. Pour in the wine, add the anchovy fillets,
a seasoning of black pepper and a pinch of cayenne. Cook gently for about 30 minutes, then rub
through a sieve, discarding any debris.

    To finish, melt the butter in a clean pan and stir in the flour to make a roux. Cook gently until
the mixture turns a golden brown. Stir in the stock and bring to a simmer to thicken the mixture.
Then add the red wine mixture and allow the sauce to cook very gently for about 30 minutes. Taste,
add more seasoning if necessary (the anchovy will probably make it salty enough) and finish with the
redcurrant jelly.

Leftovers

Venison from a prime cut can be delicious cold. Serve it with Cumberland sauce (page 144), and Watercress Salad (page 156). For reheating, Poivrade Sauce (page 140) is useful for making a hash.

Venison Pies

For a relatively large amount of leftover venison, or to use untidy bits and pieces, mince the meat and use it in little pies – good picnic or finger food. They are nicest eaten just cooled on the day of making, but can be eaten hot from the oven or cold.

200g (7oz) cooked venison
150ml (5fl oz) leftover gravy
    or Poivrade Sauce
salt and pepper
shortcrust pastry made with 75g (3oz) fat
    and 150g (5oz) plain flour

Makes 18 pies

Remove any fat and sinews from the venison and mince the meat fairly fine. Mix it with the gravy. Taste and add a little more seasoning if necessary, especially if the pies are to be eaten cold, as the flavour comes across less then.

Preheat the oven to 190°C, 375°F, Gas mark 5. Roll the pastry out thin and stamp out 18 circles for the bottom crust of the pies. Use them to line patty tins and divide the venison mixture between them. Gather the pastry trimmings, re-roll and cut 18 slightly smaller circles for the tops. Cover and press down lightly to seal the edges.

Bake for 15 minutes, or until the pastry is golden brown.

Sauces, Sides and Vegetables

Bread Sauce

A traditional accompaniment for poultry and game birds in English cookery. Recipes vary in the flavourings – nutmeg and mace appear in some, and onions are more usual than shallots. Be guided by personal taste and family tradition.

300ml (10fl oz) full-cream milk
2 cloves
75g (3oz) shallots, peeled

75g (3oz) fine breadcrumbs made from slightly stale white bread
3 tablespoons single cream
salt and pepper

Serves 4

Put the milk in the top half of a double boiler or a bowl over simmering water. Stick the cloves into the shallots and leave to infuse for about 1 hour. Strain, discarding the shallots. Return the flavoured milk to the pan or bowl and stir in the breadcrumbs. Place over hot water again for about 10–15 minutes, during which the sauce should thicken up (not too much – if necessary add a little hot milk). Taste and add a little salt and pepper. Stir in the cream and serve.

A Sauce for Cold Meat

The original of this was given as 'A sauce for Partridge, or Moor Game' in the pompously named Culina Famulatrix Medicinæ *published by Ignotus (otherwise known as Dr A Hunter) in 1807. It produces a surprisingly modern result, and is also delicious with roast meat.*

4 salted anchovies, well rinsed
2 fat garlic cloves, peeled
juice of ½ lemon (you may not need all this)

180ml (6fl oz) olive oil
cold roast meat, cut in small, neat pieces
freshly ground black pepper

Serves 4

Put the anchovies, garlic, half the lemon juice and the oil in a blender and whizz together. Taste, and add more lemon juice if you wish; you might also like to add some pepper, although it is unlikely that any salt will be needed.

Mix with the roast meat. Serve this on a bed of salad leaves or with lightly cooked French beans, or broccoli spears, or small new potatoes.

Cumberland Sauce

A delicious sauce for cold ham or game. It appears to have no links with the county of that name, and a legend associating it with the royal title of the Duke of Cumberland appears to be just that – a legend. The base of redcurrant jelly and wine is reminiscent of 18th-century sauces for venison, but the first recognisable recipe was given (under a different name) by Alexis Soyer in 1853. It seems to have been the French chef Georges Auguste Escoffier who popularised the recipe and made it a commercial success in the 19th century.

zest of 1 orange (preferably unwaxed), cut in thin strips
zest of 1 lemon (preferably unwaxed), cut in thin strips
4 tablespoons redcurrant jelly
4 tablespoons port
1 teaspoon smooth Dijon mustard
a pinch of ground ginger

Serves 4–6

Put the orange and lemon zest in a small bowl, then cover with boiling water and leave to blanch for 3–4 minutes. Drain well.

Melt the jelly in a small pan, stirring to smooth out any lumps. Add the port and mix well. Stir in the zest, the mustard and a little ginger. Taste and add a little more mustard or ginger if desired. Allow to cool before serving with cold meat.

Right: Cumberland Sauce.

Apple Sauce

Apple sauce is a traditional accompaniment for pork and goose. It is very simple to
make: peel and core 2 large Bramley apples, then cut into small pieces. Cook gently
in a small pan with just enough water to prevent them from sticking. Stir frequently.
Once they have become a purée, add about 3 teaspoons sugar, or to taste.

Caramelised Apples

*These are good served with pork, goose or duck. If serving with duck, add a little grated
orange zest at the end. The apples must be a firm-fleshed type that will keep their shape
when cooked.*

30g (1oz) unsalted butter
3 large apples (Cox's or a dryish, aromatic eating apple),
   peeled, cored and sliced, but not too thinly
a piece of star anise (optional)
1 dessertspoon cider vinegar
2 tablespoons sugar

Serves 4–6

Melt the butter in a heavy frying pan and add the apple slices, and the star anise if using. Cook
gently, stirring frequently, until the apple is softening and has become slightly transparent. Add the
cider vinegar, then the sugar and continue to cook until the apple begins to caramelise. Serve tepid.

Left: Caramelised Apples.

Red Onion 'Marmalade'

A simple take on a modern classic, to eat warm with plain roast duck.

30g (1oz) unsalted butter
1 red onion, peeled, cut in half and sliced thinly
1 tablespoon sweet sherry
2 tablespoons red wine vinegar
a piece of star anise
20g (¾oz) light soft brown sugar
salt and pepper

Serves 4

Melt the butter in a small heavy frying pan. Add the onion, cover and cook very gently for about 30 minutes, stirring occasionally. They should become soft and translucent, but not brown.

Add the sherry and let it bubble a moment, then add the wine vinegar and a piece of star anise and bring the mixture to the boil. Stir in the sugar, season with a little salt and pepper, and simmer gently, stirring frequently, for another 15–20 minutes, or until it has achieved the consistency of runny jam. Remove the star anise before serving.

Serve freshly made as an accompaniment to roast duck, or with goose or pork.

Cucumber Sauce

Cooked cucumber was popular in the 18th century, and was often served with roast mutton. The original recipe, 'To make a Salpicon for Roast Meats, as Beef, Mutton, Veal or Lamb', was recorded by John Thacker in The Art of Cookery *(1758). A salpicon is a mixture of chopped ingredients bound in a thick sauce, then used as a garnish or stuffing; make it a little more liquid and it becomes a sauce. It also works as a vehicle for leftover meat. Do use good stock to make this.*

Thacker suggests, 'You may add Sweetbreads, Morels, Trufles, Lamb stones [testicles] and pallets, Coxcombs, Mushrooms, or any of these that you can get.'

½ **cucumber, peeled, the seeds removed and**
  the flesh cut into 5mm (¼in) dice
½ **small onion, peeled and finely chopped**
250ml (9fl oz) red wine vinegar
30g (1oz) unsalted butter
a little ham or lean unsmoked bacon, finely chopped (optional)
2 tablespoons plain flour
250ml (9fl oz) good meaty stock or gravy
salt and pepper

Serves 4

Put the cucumber, onion and vinegar in a small bowl and leave to soak for 1 hour. Drain, discarding the vinegar, and blot the vegetables dry on kitchen paper.

Melt the butter in a frying pan. If you are using ham or bacon, add it at this stage and allow it to brown a little. Then add the onion and cucumber and cook briskly until they are starting to brown slightly.

Stir in the flour, then gradually add the stock, stirring to produce a sauce about the thickness of double cream. Taste and add salt and pepper as necessary, and serve with plain roast lamb or mutton.

If making this with leftovers, any gravy left from the roast can be used in place of part of the stock. Add the leftover meat, sliced, right at the end and allow it to heat through gently (if the sauce becomes very thick, add a little more stock, or water if nothing else is available).

Sage and Onion Stuffing

*This recipe – suitable for pork, goose or duck – was considered old-fashioned by the 1840s.
It was also thought too overpowering by Victorian cooks, although Eliza Acton remarked that
some people always liked it with leg of pork (which was stuffed at the knuckle end). It has
outlived Victorians and remains one of the most iconic mixtures in the English kitchen.*

*In her otherwise excellent recipe on which the one below is based, Mrs Roundell in
Mrs Roundell's Practical Cookery Book (1898), suggested that a very few well-blanched
sage leaves were sufficient. We are accustomed to much bigger flavours, so I have added a few
more and omitted the blanching.*

*A mixture based on one onion is about the right amount for stuffing a duck; double it
for a goose.*

1 large onion, peeled
12 fresh sage leaves, washed
60g (2½oz) stale breadcrumbs
20g (¾oz) unsalted butter, cut in small pieces
   (or beef suet for a traditional mixture)
1 medium egg, beaten
¼ teaspoon salt
a little freshly ground black pepper

Serves 4–6

Put the onion in a pan, cover with boiling water and simmer for 20–30 minutes, or until tender.
Drain. Once it is cool enough to handle, cut it into quarters. Put it in a food processor with the
sage and chop (but don't reduce it to a purée), or chop together by hand until fairly fine. Stir in
the breadcrumbs, butter and enough egg to bind lightly, then stir in the seasoning (don't use the
processor, which makes the mixture too runny).

Use to stuff a boned and rolled pork roast or a bird, or press into a greased dish and bake along
with the roast for the last 30 minutes of cooking time.

Vegetable Dishes

Boulangère Potatoes

A dish of French origin, popularised in Britain during the love affair with French food in the mid-20th century. Marcel Boulestin gave an early version in his book Simple French Cooking for English Homes *(1930). It is similar to* tiesen nionod, *a Welsh dish of onions and potatoes baked together like a gratin.*

2 large onions, peeled and thinly sliced
unsalted butter, for frying and for greasing the dish
about 750g (1lb 10oz) baking potatoes, peeled
150ml (5fl oz) well-flavoured stock
salt and pepper

Serves 4-6

Preheat the oven to 180–190°C, 350–375°F, Gas mark 4–5. Fry the onions gently in butter to soften them, but don't let them colour (they can be blanched in boiling water if you prefer). Slice the potatoes thinly.

Grease a shallow ovenproof dish with butter and arrange the potatoes and onions in layers, seasoning well as you go. Finish with a neat layer of overlapping potato slices. Dot with butter and pour in the stock; it should come almost to the top of the dish.

Bake in the oven until the potatoes are soft and the surface nicely browned. A little extra (hot) stock or water can be added during cooking if the dish seems to be drying out, but this dish is better for not swimming in liquid.

Potatoes Roast in Cream and Herbs

This is not a traditional method for roasting potatoes, but it is good with just about any meat, especially game.

2–3 fresh rosemary sprigs about
    6cm (2½in) long
8–10 fresh sage leaves
12 fresh thyme sprigs
1–2 garlic cloves, peeled

750g (1lb 10oz) potatoes, peeled
    and cut in 2cm (¾in) chunks
200ml (7fl oz) double cream
1 teaspoon salt
freshly ground black pepper

Serves 4–6

Preheat the oven to 200°C, 400°F, Gas mark 6.

Strip the leaves off the rosemary and chop them together with the sage, thyme and garlic. Mix the potatoes, cream, chopped herb mixture, salt and some pepper. Put them in an ovenproof dish or small roasting tin that holds them comfortably in a shallow layer.

Cook for about 30 minutes, stirring once or twice. By the end of this time, they should be tender (give them a little longer if not), and the cream should be thick, clinging to the potatoes and lightly flecked with gold on the surface.

Mashed Potatoes

I can't remember where I first came across this version, but I think it was in a 19th-century book and the writer stated that it was the way the French made mashed potato.

500g (1lb 2oz) potatoes
30g (1oz) unsalted butter
salt and pepper

Serves 4

Peel the potatoes, then cut into chunks and boil as usual. When tender, do not pour the cooking water down the sink, but drain it into a jug.

Add the butter to the potatoes and season with salt and pepper. Mash the potatoes, adding a little of the reserved cooking water and continuing to mash, adding more cooking water if necessary, or butter if you want, until you feel they have achieved the right consistency.

Roast Potatoes

Roast potatoes are a defining element of 'a proper roast'. King Edward, a potato variety with almost iconic status in Britain, probably has the best flavour, and can develop a fantastic crisp crust and melting interior. Wilja and Desirée are also good; Cara and Romano should produce reasonable results.

1kg (2¼lb) potatoes
about 50g (2oz) fat for roasting, such as beef or pork dripping
salt

Serves 4-6

The oven needs to be hot – 200–220°C, 400–425°F, Gas mark 6–7. Peel the potatoes. Leave small ones whole, and cut large ones into smaller pieces (3–4 each). Put them in a pan, just cover with cold water and bring to the boil. Boil for 5–7 minutes. Tip them into a colander and drain well.

Put the fat in a roasting tin and place in the oven to melt and get very hot. Take it out and add the potatoes. (Wear oven gloves and an apron in case the fat spits – it should be hot enough to sizzle satisfactorily.) Turn the potatoes well in the hot fat, sprinkle with salt and roast for 40–50 minutes. In a gas oven, put the potatoes at the top. Turn once or twice during cooking, and add a little more salt each time.

Cabbage

1 pointed cabbage or Savoy cabbage
about 15g (½oz) unsalted butter,
    bacon fat or olive oil

a few juniper berries, bruised
1–2 tablespoons cider vinegar
salt

Serves 4

Trim the cabbage leaves of their central stalk, wash and shred the leaves. Put them in a pan with a well-fitting lid. The water clinging to the leaves after washing should be enough, or add 2–3 tablespoons. Add the butter, juniper berries and a little salt. Put the lid on the pan and put it on the lowest heat for about 15 minutes. Look occasionally to make sure that the cabbage isn't drying up; add a small amount of water if it is. When just tender, add the cider vinegar, mix well and serve.

Red Cabbage

1 generous tablespoon goose,
    pork or bacon fat, or oil
1 medium onion, peeled
    and roughly chopped
1–2 apples, preferably sourish ones,
    peeled, cored and chopped
1 small red cabbage, quartered,
    stem removed, finely sliced

2–3 tablespoons cider vinegar
2 tablespoons light pale brown sugar
4–5 cloves, bruised
5cm (2in) cinnamon stick
1 piece of orange zest (preferably
    unwaxed) about 5 x 2cm (2 x 1in)
1 teaspoon salt
freshly ground black pepper

Serves 6

Preheat the oven to 140°C, 275°F, Gas mark 1. Heat the fat in an ovenproof casserole and fry the onion until translucent. Stir in the apples, then the cabbage and fry lightly for a few minutes. Add the other ingredients and stir well. Cover and transfer to the oven for about 1½ hours. This can be cooked on the hob, but the heat must be very low – and stir frequently, adding a little more water from time to time if it shows signs of drying up.

Right: Red Cabbage.
Next page: Roast Potatoes.

Roast Parsnips

This is a root that goes well with roast beef. Parsnips are considered to be at their best in winter, after the first frosts – freezing temperatures convert some of the starch in the living roots into sugar, and this caramelises when they are cooked. Look for ones that are fresh and firm; flabby parsnips don't cook well.

**about 50g (2oz) fat for roasting, such as dripping
from beef or pork or lard
about 500g (1–1½lb) parsnips
salt**

Serves 4–6

The method for cooking these is similar to that for Roast Potatoes (see page 151). Wash and trim the parsnips and scrape off the skin with a peeler. Cut, on the diagonal, into slices about 5mm (¼in) thick. They can be parboiled for about 5 minutes, but if they are good and fresh, this isn't necessary. Put the fat in a roasting tin in a hot oven at 220°C, 425°F, Gas mark 7.

Drain the parsnips well if parboiled, then tip into the hot fat (protect your hands with oven gloves). Turn them around in the fat, sprinkle with a little salt and roast for 10 minutes. Turn the heat down to 190°C, 375°F, Gas mark 5 and cook for another 20–30 minutes, stirring occasionally so that they develop nicely browned surfaces. Drain well before serving.

Left: Roast Parsnips.
Previous page: Ragoo of Onions and Mushrooms.

Ragoo of Onions and Mushrooms

'Ragoo' was the 18th-century English cook's phonetic rendition of the French ragoût. *Complex mixtures requiring two or three different meaty stocks, these dishes were all the rage at the time. They were used as sauces and garnishes, or could be dishes in their own right. This one is good with white meat poultry of all sorts – and can also be served with beef, mutton or game. A good meaty stock based on chicken or veal, plus some ham, bacon or gammon is essential.*

2 tablepoons olive oil
1 small onion, peeled and very finely chopped
1 celery stick, trimmed and very finely chopped
1 medium carrot, trimmed and very finely chopped
100g (4oz) lean unsmoked bacon or gammon, very finely chopped
400ml (14fl oz) well-flavoured stock
a bouquet garni of fresh parsley, thyme, marjoram (optional)
400g (14oz) shallots or very small onions, peeled
200g (7oz) button mushrooms, trimmed
salt and pepper

Serves 4

Heat the oil in a saucepan. Add the onion, celery and carrot and fry briskly, stirring frequently until the vegetables begin to caramelise and turn golden brown at the edges. Add the bacon and continue to fry for another 5–10 minutes. Any trimmings from the mushrooms can be added too. Pour in the stock, then add the bouquet garni. Once the mixture has come to the boil, turn it to the lowest possible simmer and leave to cook until reduced by about half.

Put the shallots and mushrooms in a clean pan. Strain the reduced stock over them, pressing so that all the flavoursome juices pass through (but don't rub any of the solids through). Continue to cook very gently, stirring from time to time. By the time the onions are tender (about 45 minutes), the stock should be reduced to a few spoonfuls of thick, slightly syrupy liquid, just coating the vegetables. Taste and adjust the seasoning.

Crisp Fried Browned Onions

Useful as a garnish for all sorts of leftover meat and potato dishes, and good in cold beef sandwiches (see page 29). It may take a couple of goes to master this, but it's worth the effort.

sunflower oil, for frying
1 large onion, peeled, halved lengthways and sliced very thinly

Serves 2–4 as a garnish

Line a plate or small tray with a few sheets of kitchen paper. Heat a layer of oil about 1cm (½in) deep in a frying pan (a heavy cast-iron one is best). Add the onions and regulate the heat so that they cook fairly fast. Partially cover the pan, so that there is a small gap for steam to escape. You will need to remove the lid and stir them fairly frequently, to make sure they cook evenly. Don't let them brown patchily.

When the onions start to look shrunken and are beginning to brown, leave the lid off and stir constantly. They should begin to brown quite rapidly; at this point, watch them closely. You want them to be brown, not burnt. When they begin to change colour to a deeper, caramel brown, turn off the heat and remove them immediately with a slotted spoon. Scatter them over the kitchen paper to absorb any remaining oil.

Watercress Salad

A salad of watercress has a long history of accompanying roast birds at table. Served with duck, it usually had orange segments added, but if pomegranates are available, I think they are better.

2 bunches of watercress,
    washed and picked over
the seeds of ½ pomegranate (or
    use the segments of 2 oranges –
    cut off the pith with a small,
    sharp knife)

FOR THE DRESSING
scant 1 teaspoon smooth
    Dijon mustard
1 tablespoon wine vinegar
4–5 tablespoons olive oil
salt and pepper

Serves 4

For the dressing, mix the mustard and vinegar together, then season to taste. Stir in the oil. Toss the watercress with the dressing, then scatter with the pomegranate and serve at once.

Puréed Brussels Sprouts

During the early 1980s, it seemed that all vegetables had to be served as purées, a fashion derived from the then influential French nouvelle cuisine. They have mostly had their moment and gone, but Brussels sprouts are good done this way and go very well with game birds.

500g (1lb 2oz) Brussels sprouts, trimmed
125ml (4fl oz) single cream
salt and pepper

Serves 4

Cook the sprouts in boiling water until tender. Drain well. Process with the cream and add seasoning to taste. Don't overdo the processing – you should be left with a beautiful pale green purée, lightly flecked with darker green, like a piece of jade.

Chestnut Gratin

An accompaniment to game birds that is also good for turkey. Peeling chestnuts is tedious,
but the results are lighter and fresher-tasting than using tinned purée.

600g (1¼lb) chestnuts in their shells
300ml (10fl oz) stock (appropriate to the roast),
   or chicken stock or milk
30g (1oz) unsalted butter
3 tablespoons dry breadcrumbs
3 tablespoons grated Parmesan cheese
salt

Serves 4–6

Cut a slit in the shell of each chestnut and cook them in boiling water for about 15 minutes. Take off the heat, remove them from the water a few at a time, and when just cool enough to handle, peel off the brown outer shells and the inner membrane. Return the shelled chestnuts to a clean pan and cover with the stock. Simmer gently until very tender, then pass the whole lot through a sieve to make a purée.

Preheat the oven to 200°C, 400°F, Gas mark 6.

Beat the butter into the chestnuts, add a pinch of salt, and pour into a buttered gratin dish. Mix the breadcrumbs with the Parmesan and scatter over the top. Brown in the oven for about 15 minutes.

Index

Further Reading

Acton, Eliza, *Modern Cookery for Private Families*, 1855 edition with an introduction by Elizabeth Ray (Southover Press, 1993)

Beeton, Isabella, *Beeton's Book of Household Management*, 1861 edition (Chancellor Press, London 1982)

Bradley, Martha, *The British Housewife*, 1756 edition with an introduction by Gilly Lehmann (Prospect Books, 1996)

Cobbett, Anne, *The English Housekeeper* (1840)

Davidson, Alan, *The Oxford Companion to Food* (Oxford University Press, 1999)

Dickson Wright, Clarissa, and Johnny Scott, *Sunday Roast* (Kyle Cathie, 2006)

Edington, Sarah, *Complete Traditional Recipe Book* (National Trust Books, 2006)

Fearnley-Whittingstall, Hugh, *The River Cottage Meat Book* (Hodder and Stoughton, 2004)

Kenney-Herbert, Colonel, *Common-Sense Cookery* (Edward Arnold, 1905)

Luke, Harry, (edited by Peter and Michael Luke), *The Tenth Muse* (The Rubicon Press, 1992)

Paston-Williams, Sara, *Good Old-Fashioned Jams, Preserves and Chutneys* (National Trust Books, 2008)

Rogers, Ben, *Beef and Liberty* (Chatto and Windus, 2003)

Thacker, John, *The Art of Cookery*, 1758 edition with an introduction by Ivan Day (Southover Press, 2004)

Appetite for Change

Food is much more than what we eat. It shapes our lives – our health and well-being, our culture, our natural environment, our security and prosperity. Food is a true measure of our approach to life itself, as individuals and as a society.

At the National Trust, we are passionate about good food – it is integral to our past, present and future. The full story of food from plot to plate is intimately represented in the places in our care, inspiring the millions of people who visit every year. Our gardeners, chefs, tenant farmers and others have daily experience of the realities of producing and preparing food in the 21st century.

The National Trust owns 250,000 hectares of land across England, Northern Ireland and Wales, more than 80 per cent of which is used to produce food, working with 1,500 tenant farmers. Food production on our land ranges from large-scale tenant-run commercial farms to kitchen gardens, allotments and orchards. Our 150 restaurants and tea-rooms serve over 8 million people every year. We have a unique perspective that spans the historic, natural, social and economic impacts of food. Over 75 per cent of Trust farms are in environmental stewardship schemes, which reward the conservation of nature and the wider environment, and provide access to the countryside. 26 of our historic kitchen gardens are in production and supply their restaurants and tea-rooms with fresh fruit and vegetables. We own over 100 traditional orchards producing a huge variety of fruit and nuts. We grow in ways that reduce our environmental impact, with careful use of water, using peat-free compost and with minimal use of artificial chemicals. We have 145 walled gardens, many with huge potential to be restored to food production.

In 2009 the National Trust launched a long-term plan to get local communities involved and hand over space for allotments to 'grow your own'. Our main aim is to help those who are new to growing to find the space they need and help them learn how and what to grow. National Trust gardeners and garden volunteers will be able to share their skills and knowledge with the community.

Farm Foods for Sale

Some of the most-visited National Trust properties are now holding regular farmers' and food markets, including Stourhead and Lacock Abbey in Wiltshire, Waddesdon Manor in Buckinghamshire, Sissinghurst in Kent and Dunster Castle in Somerset. In addition, many National Trust properties or tenants sell direct to the public via farmers' markets, locally or online.

Visit www.nationaltrust.org.uk/food to find out more.